Once We

A Journey with Africa's

Texts

Dhyani Berger

Chenjerai Hove

Margaret Jacobsohn

Antjie Krog

Gcina Mhlope

Victor Munnik

Paul Ntiati

Sérgio Veiga

Tony Weaver

Photography

Paul Weinberg

Were Hunters

Indigenous People

Mets & Schilt, Amsterdam

Novib, 's-Gravenhage / 11.11.11-uitgeverij, Brussel

David Philip, Cape Town

Contents

Photographer's foreword

By Paul Weinberg

In the shade of a Mopane tree in a dry river bed in the heart of Koakaveld, Namibia, a Himba elder by the name of Wapenga, asks me a question. His eyes are challenging. He is dressed in elegant Himba gear. His hair is platted and shaped, held in place with a stocking. Around his neck he wears a thick metal necklace pasted with mud. He has tyre sandals on his feet and he is carrying a stick. In the background are the roofs of a small settlement made of mud and thatch, not far from his own. The landscape is hot, dry and stony, punctuated with patches of yellow grass. In the stark, midday light the soil shines silvery from the volcanic deposits of another ecological period.

'What is the way forward?' he asks.

I am struck by the significance of the question. Here I am, at the cusp of the millennium, visiting a group of people living as they have done for thousands of years. But in the last century the world around Wapenga and his people has dramatically changed. He sees tourists drive past in smart cars en route to further places. Sometimes they stop to take photographs or ask the way. He watches their tracks in the sand and the dust settle. They come from a world that is surging forward at a furious pace. We call it 'progress', 'development', 'globalisation'. They come to Wapenga's world to temporarily escape

their world. They call it 'ecotourism', 'travel', 'safari'.

For Wapenga, his world is much like the world his forebears knew. His paramount concerns are about the management of his herd, his wealth, his culture. His survival is about co-existing with nature and living off the land.

Where does Wapenga's and the tourists' worlds meet and what is their relationship to each other? What do they learn and benefit from each other? What do I say to Wapenga? His question is the one I wanted to ask him. In fact it is the question that sparked off this whole journey.

But this is Africa, the day is young and we drink tea. This is my last trip for this book. I have traveled over 50 000 kilometres in six different countries, worked with nine different writers, all wrestling with 'way forward' issues, researching, listening and gaining wisdom.

I should have something to say. I tell him about what I have seen. In Kenya the Maasai have cultural villages where people pay to visit and buy crafts. I tell him of a new game farm in Botswana that is owned by the San. Here you pay to go on walks and learn the crafts of the San as has been passed down for thousands of years. I tell him of villagers in Zimbabwe who benefit from hunting. Professional hunters get concessions to hunt wildlife, in return the local people receive meat and a pay-out at the end of the year.

We continue to drink tea. Wapenga says he likes what the Maasai have done. He says he would like elephant, rhino and zebra here in Kaokaveld because their children do not know these animals and animals attract tourism. He tells me not everyone has the same point of view. His Himba neighbours to the east prefer to kill their tourist assets, their wildlife. He sees no future with these people and will leave them out of his plans.

We fall silent for a while. I am struck by the complexity of the issues. I search for answers for

Wapenga, travelling back in my mind, scanning the journey. From place to place, country to country, Wapenga's simple but crucial question elicits different answers. Each country has a different conservation policy, each region a contrasting set of ecological, political, economic and social dynamics. In Kenya, local people live side by side with wildlife; the wild herds grazing alongside the domestic ones. There are no fences and there is no hunting. Indigenous people own the game reserves. In South Africa there are fences and indigenous people live outside most of the reserves. Debates about how indigenous communities can benefit from wildlife and contribute to its conservation are not yet settled in this new democracy. In Zimbabwe, hunting is the key income-earner for many local people. In Mozambique, now free from civil war, tourists are flocking back but without proper conservation management, this beautiful environment is under threat. Locals and tourists compete for the natural resources, especially the sea life, the former for pleasure, the latter for survival.

Wapenga1s country, Namibia, has a very progressive policy which allows local people, like himself, to declare a conservancy. Once a conservancy has been established, interested parties may approach the local people and propose a partnership to set up a lodge, safari operation or a hunting concession. Three hundred kilometres to the south of where we sit is the conservancy of Torra in Damaraland. It is a shining example of local people's control of resources and business relationships. They have now established a trust, the monies being used for a wide range of community initiatives: from education bursaries to boreholes.

Wapenga's question is echoed throughout the African landscape by millions of its indigenous people. In essence it asks how indigenous people may benefit from the resources they have curated all these years. In Botswana, whose beautiful natural heritage goes a long way to keeping the country stable and wealthy, one of the local leaders, Chief Tawana, is outspoken about this issue. As a traditional and historical custodian of the Okavango swamps – which boasts some of Africa's finest natural resources and private game reserves – he recently urged a conference of indigenous people to stand up for their rights. 'Don't we deserve a cut?' he asked.

What is the way forward? Underpinning Wapenga's question are anxieties shared by many indigenous people we visited on this journey. Will his people's rights to land be secured? Will he get a fair deal out of tourism? Will becoming world-wise and educated mean a loss of tradition? Will the elders lose their power and limited wealth?

In the shade of the Mopane tree everything seems relaxed and just like another day. But we both know there are deep issues here and they need answers.

Kxao Moses, a Bushmen and the manager of the Ju'wasi natural resources in Bushmanland, Namibia, knows this problem well. He has seen his grandfather and his father lose their birthright, the land, in the name of colonialism, apartheid and conservation. Each system was designed to reduce the size of their land. Kxao Moses is educated and eloquent and has spent much of his life addressing activists in Africa and the rest of the world, sharing his people's struggles with other indigenous groups and concerned organisations. Kxao Moses has a dream that one day his people will stand strong again: 'My dream is to see the day when we can stand up and say 'We have all the rights to our land'; when we can stand up and say 'We can do all things for ourselves, we don't need donors, we can survive on our own, from the land, from the environment, just like in the old days before the white man came.'

It is my hope that Wapenga and Kxao Moses will be able to meet and work out some answers between themselves and with many others who ask the same question: 'What is the way forward?'

'*In the olden days,*' said Kxao, '*the times were very good, they were very very good. Today we have gone back, back, back, backwards, we have been put down, why, why? That time long ago when we were alone, when there were no whites, no army, no politics, when it was just us Bushman people, we fixed everything ourselves, then the white people came and brought politics here.*'

Kxao, Nyae Nyae Conservancy, Bushmanland (Namibia)

Kalahari, Namibia and Botswana

No respite for the San

*By Tony Weaver**

We arrived at Tsumkwe Lodge just after sunset. Our host, Arno Oosthuysen, told us that *National Geographic* had booked several rooms. Paul and I groaned. We'd been planning a nice, quiet trip, and here we had the big-budget boys on our backs. 'It's been hectic,' Arno continued. 'Last week we had a BBC film crew; the week before it was the French.'

That's the San of southern Africa. They are among the most filmed, photographed and written about people on earth. But they are also among the most marginalised, pulled in all directions by political and military forces beyond their control. The celebrated ethnographic filmmaker John Marshall once wrote an article on the San entitled 'Death by myth'. It remains one of the most telling descriptions of the plight of the First People of Africa.

The *National Geographic* crew arrived. We were expecting the worst – Americans with no local knowledge and a huge budget, ready to romanticise the last of the Bushmen. Instead, in

walked my old friend, the author and journalist Peter Godwin, and Chris Johns, one of the world's finest nature and wildlife photographers. 'I suspect,' said Peter after our fourth single malt, 'that the story we're going to find will be one of either great tragedy or great hope.' He was right on both scores.

Tsumkwe (Tjum!kui) is the capital of what was once called eastern Bushmanland, just about the last place where the San – in this case the Ju/'hoansi (pronounced ZhoonKwazee) – control their own land. I first came here with John Marshall in 1984. At that time it was a terrible place. Most of the men had been recruited into the South African and South West African armies. They were receiving cash wages for the first time in their lives, and this and other changes were wreaking havoc with the local community; alcoholism, murder, wife-beating and child neglect – all forms of behaviour traditionally alien to the San – had become commonplace.

Most of the Ju/'hoansi were living in Tsumkwe in miserable fibreglass and asbestos igloo huts provided by the government. One small group of diehards still lived in the bush, at a place called /Aotcha (pronounced Gautsha), trying to hunt and gather, stay out of the grasp of the army, and keep the old traditions alive.

Author's note: I freely interchange the words San, Basarwa, Bushmen and other terms. Strictly speaking, none of them are politically correct. If the various agencies involved with the Bushmen spent less time being politically correct and more time fighting the good fight, this story wouldn't be happening today.

It has been a long and difficult process, but today almost all the Ju/'hoansi are back at their traditional *n!ores*, the areas where they have hereditary hunting and gathering rights. The entire former Bushmanland has been proclaimed as the Nyae Nyae Conservancy, a vast, unfenced game and nature reserve which the Ju/'hoansi control.

Structures are still pretty informal, but you can go there and spend a day or a week in the bush with the old hunters, gathering veld food and tracking game. Arno told us that a German guest had just spent a week in the veld with one of the old hunters, carrying a backpack, water purifier and sleeping bag.

He reckoned this pointed to a fine line the conservancy would have to walk. 'Tourism is not the only answer for this region. Yes, it will help the San to look at their culture and rediscover it, but it is a difficult balance. The Bushmen are not caged baboons for the tourists to stare at.

'The first question tourists ask me is, "Where can we see the Bushmen?" I say, you've just

driven through town, and the people you saw are Bushmen. "But they aren't wearing skins," the tourists complain. They are chasing an image, an illusion, and we as tourism vendors are selling that image and that illusion.

'Only the older men dress in traditional clothes these days. In the first world they are big losers; they don't have the life skills to cope with autobanks and cars and alcohol and all that stuff. But go into the bush with them and they own that world; you will never die in the bush with a Bushman.'

The next morning we made an arrangement to go on what is described here as 'the Bushman experience'. The idea is that you go into the bush with the Ju/'hoansi and track game, gather veld food, and get an idea of what their culture is all about. We stopped at the village of De#Uha near Klein Dobe to set up the deal. 'Do you want us to wear our normal clothes or skins?' an old man called Kxao Xexe asked us. We were a little taken aback. 'Uh, just wear whatever you feel

Landmark agreement in South Africa

Meanwhile, in the southern Kalahari, events surrounding the San and their ties with the land appear to have taken a more positive turn. In an historic agreement signed in March 1999, the South African government gave the ≠Khomani San ownership of a portion of the Kalahari Gemsbok National Park, a large game park in the extreme north west of the country bordering on Namibia and Botswana. In terms of the agreement, the first of its kind in the country, land use in this 'contract park' will remain unchanged, but the San will gain cultural and commercial rights to the territory. While many of the details remain to be finalised, South African National Parks will probably continue to manage the park while the community prepares to take over these functions.

The ≠Khomani San is one of four San groupings once found in South Africa; while the others are effectively extinct, about 500 ≠Khomani survive. The ≠Khomani were acknowledged to have residential status in the Kalahari Gemsbok National Park when it was first proclaimed in 1931. Nevertheless, from 1937 onwards efforts were made to expel them from the park. In the mid-1970s the ≠Khomani were reclassified as 'coloured' in terms of apartheid laws, and removed from the park. Many became farm workers in the adjacent Mier district (a 'coloured' reserve), while others were scattered throughout the subcontinent. In the intervening years the clan became impoverished, and lost its language and culture. Anthropologists believed the N/u language had become extinct, but in the 1990s 11 speakers of the language and a related dialect, !Kabee, were discovered.

Following South Africa's transition to democracy, the ≠Khomani, assisted by NGOs, claimed ownership of the entire park under the new government's restitution laws. Eventually, the authorities agreed to relinquish control over an area of 55 000 hectares. This area will be halved between the San and the Mier community, which also lost land to the park.

The San will live on farms to the south of the park, to be bought from the Mier community; the Mier will be compensated with 30 000 hectares of substitute land added to the Mier commonage.

The land restitution process has been extremely important for the ≠Khomani San, linking all the scattered groupings and giving them a sense of common identity. The signing ceremony brought the entire community together for the first time in decades, including the last 11 speakers of the N/u language. While few doubt the significance of the agreement in principle, opinions differ on its outcome in practice. First, doubts centre on the group's ability to manage the park. The leaders of a major ≠Khomani grouping have declared that they intend to recreate their lives as hunter-gatherers. This does not seem feasible; expanding their existing skills of engaging with tourism seems to be a more practicable route.

If the ≠Khomani are to manage the park, the various groupings will have to agree on a common approach. However, indications are that the community remains divided.

Doubts also centre on the parks board's will or capacity to implement the agreement; little has happened in practice since it was signed. Nevertheless, the agreement has at least created the potential for a new departure. Petrus Vaalbooi, who chairs the Southern Kalahari San Association, has commented: 'I feel very positive now. A year ago I wouldn't have said this. But from the words I hear now, I believe we have nearly crossed the bridge. I don't believe that land will solve the problems of the San, but at least we have a future and a life. We will be the owners of our own land.'

References Crawhall, Nigel. 1999. 'Reclaiming rights, resources and identity: the power of an ancient San language' in *Voices, Values and Identities Symposium,* Ed. Yvonne Dladla. Pretoria: South African National Parks.
'San Celebration', 1999. Timbila: *Rhythms of the Earth [South African National Parks magazine]* 1 (2): 16-17.
Jacklyn Cock and David Fig. 1999. *From colonial to community-based conservation: environmental justice and the national parks of South Africa.*

comfortable wearing on a normal tourist outing,' we eventually replied.

We came back after lunch. Kxao and a tiny, wizened hunter called G!wi Kxao were waiting for us. Together with Kxao Xexe's wife, Bê Kxao, and G!wi's son, Debe Toma, we wandered off into the veld. The men were dressed in traditional beaded skins. Bê Kxao was dressed in a mix of old and new, and Debe Toma was wearing army castoffs.

Their eyes never stopped moving. Our interpreter, John !Xu Nani, kept up a running translation. 'This is the root called *dunga*, we roast it in the fire, this tsamma melon is where we find liquid and food, this berry is called *!ni*, it is very good for vitamins and juice. We call this root devil's claw, you shave and squeeze it and water comes out. This is the *kamma*, the Bushman potato, you roast that in the ashes.'

Kxao and G!wi squatted down and gathered a pile of dry grass. G!wi took two fire sticks from his PVC quiver and began to rub them together. In less than a minute he had a blaze going. (We were later told that you can tell who the real hunters are because they use PVC pipes as quivers instead of the old bark tubes – the PVC pipes keep the arrows and poison dry and stop the arrows from warping.)

As we walked, the landscape gradually came alive as we began to see it through the old hunters' eyes. Improbably, I yearned for the days when this was the only way of life.

Squatting around the fire after our bush walk, Kxao and G!wi reflected on their lives today and what they used to be when they were young men. 'In the olden days,' said Kxao, 'the times were very good, they were very very good. Today we have gone back, back, back, backwards, we have been put down, why, why? That time long ago when we were alone, when there were no whites, no army, no politics, when it was just us Bushman people, we fixed everything ourselves; then the white people came and brought politics here.'

At Baraka, headquarters of the Nyae Nyae Conservancy, piles of signboards were stacked up ready to be erected. They were part of the plan to formalise access to this wonderful near-wilderness area, where big game wander unfenced and you are as likely to see an elephant as a skunk on your bush walks. But, as with many other areas in southern Africa, uncontrolled offroad access is causing environmental and social damage. We heard stories of South African offroaders (who else?) who treat the Ju/'hoansi as part of the fauna and flora.

Kxao Moses #Oma is manager of the Nyae Nyae Conservancy, and a driving force behind the tourism plans. 'We have had many problems with tourists in the past because we didn't have any concrete controls. People just drove in, went into the villages, got people to dance, and then went away paying them just a few dollars. We are a friendly and trusting people, and so people take advantage of us.'

The conservancy has now established semi-formal campsites at designated beauty spots, specific 4x4 routes to be followed, and craft sales,

and will soon offer guided bush walks on a more formal basis than at present. Much of the process of establishing the conservancy has been driven by foreign aid and development workers, and it has often been a case of two steps forwards, one step backwards because of inter-agency feuding, inappropriate projects and personality problems.

Kxao Moses wants nothing more than to see the Ju/'hoansi take control of the process: 'My dream is to see the day when we can stand up and say, We have all the rights to our land, we can stand up and say, We can do all things for ourselves, we don't need donors, we can survive on our own, from the land, from the environment, just like in the old days before the white man came.

'I want to see the Bushmen write their own history so that we can interpret our own language, because when you are translating everything you lose things; we need to write our own history. If we make sure our kids go to school, to the tech, to university, if we adults stand up and put our heads together and combine our knowledge and skills, then the road ahead will be much better.'

Not far from Tsumkwe, but light years apart in terms of their plight, are the Kxoe San people of the Caprivi and Kavango. We drove through the Kaudom Game Reserve to get to their territory, and went in search of their community conservation and tourism project the next morning. What we found was heartbreaking.

The Kxoe have been allocated land rights on the Kavango River, just below the main falls at Popa, one of the most beautiful spots in all of Namibia. Here the community has built what must rate as one of the most exquisite campsites in southern Africa: four secluded and completely private stands, each with its own wooden deck, under deep gallery forest and perched just above the rapids. But the Kxoe have been caught up in a political struggle which is not of their making, and which has devastated their community.

Early in August 1999 the Namibian defence force swiftly put down a half-baked secessionist rebellion in Katima Mulilo. For months before this, the Namibian authorities had been accusing elements among the Kxoe of siding with the secessionists. So when the heat was turned up, the secessionist leader, Mishake Muyongo, fled into Botswana with several hundred (or thousand, depending on which report you believe) followers, and half the Kxoe people of the Caprivi went with him.

So, when we visited the campsite at the Popa Falls in June 1999, we found just a handful of people there. The authorities had cordoned off the area with razor wire which stretched from the main Caprivi highway almost down to the river, and ran over traditional Kxoe land. The few Kxoe people left were reluctant to speak. Their chief, Kibi (or Kippie) George, and his senior adviser, Thadeus Chedau, had both fled to Botswana.

The dust of the abortive rebellion will quickly settle in battered Katima Mulilo, but the consequences for the Kxoe of the Caprivi are likely to be dire. Their story is the reverse of that of the Ju/'hoansi, and I hold out little hope for them in the short term. It was with a deep sense of sadness that we left the Caprivi, heading down

through the Okavango Panhandle into Botswana to our last destination: D'Kar, home to the mainly Naro-speaking San, and the Central Kalahari Game Reserve (CKGR).

At D'Kar we visited one of the longest-running San Bushmen development projects, the Kuru Development Trust. Funded largely by Dutch and Scandinavian churches and NGOs, Kuru is an attempt to salvage remnants of the culture of the Ncoakhoe people, who once roamed most of this section of the Kalahari unhindered. But the area around Ghanzi and D'Kar is prime cattle country, and, with no regard to traditional San ownership, the land was cut up into huge ranches owned by Afrikaners, British settlers, BaKgalagadi and BaHerero.

As the fences went up, so the San became increasingly marginalised, with most becoming farm labourers on what had been their own land. Today the bulk of the people still work on the farms, or live in squalor around D'Kar and Ghanzi. But one Kuru project (it also runs leather and craft workshops and a host of other development projects) promises a future through wildlife and tourism.

The trust has bought a 7 500 hectare farm called Dqae Qare on the road from D'Kar to Ghanzi. The farm has been game-fenced, the old homestead renovated and refurbished, and five luxury bedrooms added. Besides this a campsite has been developed deep in the bush. To date 23 Naro San have been employed as guides, cooks, drivers, game guards and managers. They also form a management committee.

We went on an overnight trek with two committee members, Joseph Dii and X'aga Tshumu. With donkeys carrying our provisions and packs we meandered through the Kalahari with our guides stopping every few metres to pick veld food, point out tracks, or explain aspects of the landscape.

Our camp for the night was in a purpose-built Bushman village, with five beehive huts in a semicircle around a fireplace. I asked Joseph whether he had learnt the knowledge he was passing on to us from his forefathers. He laughed. 'Before I started working here, I was a petrol pump attendant, and before that a farm labourer. We have lost most of our knowledge, so we have regular workshops where the older people teach us about the veld and tell us traditional stories.'

As jackals yapped at the rising moon, X'aga told us some of those stories. They were fables and parables that conveyed something about morality and natural law – like the one about the jackal and the dog who were good friends, living together in the bush. One day the dog and the jackal decided they wanted to eat cooked meat, so dog went to the humans' village and found some bones and pap. He ate so well that he forgot all about jackal, and at sunset the jackal began howling: 'Ai, ai, ai, my friend, come back here.'

X'aga continued: 'But the dog said, "Life is so soft here with the people that I am staying". Then he went out hunting with the people, and he caught the jackal, and the jackal said, "Please, my friend, do not kill me, we are related". But ever

since then the jackal and the dog have been enemies.' I asked X'aga what she saw as the meaning of the story. 'If you have an old friend, and you get rich, or get food, or your life gets better, do not just throw your friend away and forget about him.'

Joseph explained that 'in our story-telling, we look for lessons about how to live our lives, how to see if people are good or evil, or which people you have to be careful of; there are lessons in every story.'

We left the farm and returned to D'Kar to talk to Mathambo NgaKaeaja, co-ordinator of the regional branch of the Working Group of Indigenous Minorities in Southern Africa (WIMSA). Mathambo was the first Naro-speaking person to obtain a university degree – a BSc in geology – and he is bitter about the way in which his people have been used by generations of settlers. While acknowledging the good done by European aid workers, he would like nothing more than to see the San of Botswana unite and develop some real political clout of their own.

'Life for us is a dynamic between traditional and cultural practices,' he remarked; 'my great-grandfather aspired to be the very best hunter, but I aspired to go to university. When you look at projects like this, you have to be very careful not to say that people should go back a hundred, 200 years just for tourism. As Bushmen we are highly marginalised, so we have to look at ways of surviving in a modern world.

'The only way forward is education and mobilisation, and if that means that the romanticised Bushman culture of the past must die, then so be it. Somewhere in the middle must be a mean where we can keep our Bushman practices and survive in the 21st century. But if it is a question of survival, then we must lose our traditions.'

Mathambo is part of an influential younger crew in San regional politics who are angry and frustrated. The San have seen academics, writers, photographers, aid workers, priests, philosophers

and filmmakers come and go and become famous on their story. Now they are dying because of their fame, and everybody is too polite and too dependent on government permits to speak out.

All except Mathambo and a handful of others: 'Don't believe that there are no more of our people living in the central Kalahari,' he declared; 'there are still more than 250 staunch people who are staying inside, who will not move out of there. This is where our people have lived since the beginning of time, for thousands and thousands of years, and they will not move.'

He was referring to the drawn-out conflict over the Botswana government's removal of San communities from the CKGR. Despite internal resistance, and intermittent international protests, this process has continued for some 20 years to the point where all San communities may have been removed from this age-old refuge – one of the last places where they had lived as hunter-gatherers.

Now, Mathambo was telling us that a handful of people were still holding out at the centre of the reserve. None of the other 'experts' in Ghanzi and D'Kar, strongholds of 'expat' aid and passive activism, seemed to have any first-hand experience of what was actually happening at places such as Molapo and Metsimanong, said to be two of the surviving settlements.

We decided to go in search of those '250 staunch people'. We could be chasing a chimera, looking for people who might no longer be there. Given that this was a 600-kilometre detour from our planned route through deep, grinding Kalahari sand, where covering 200 kilometres in six hours was speeding, it could be an expensive chimera. But we wanted to ascertain, without any doubt, the fate of the people Mathambo had spoken of.

So we left D'Kar and drove into the reserve, navigating from maps decorated with photographs of wizened Bushman hunters staring into the desert. Our guidebooks all began with phrases such as 'this ancestral hunting ground of the Bushmen'. Chris and Tilde Stuart's 1989 guide stated: 'This 51 800 square kilometre game reserve is still inhabited by groups of Bushmen, and for this reason it is closed to the general public.' Ten years later, it is very much open for business.

Veronica Roodt's *Shell Tourist Guide to Botswana*, published in February 1998, noted that 'the Central Kalahari Game Reserve ... was initially set aside primarily for the use of people who choose to continue their traditional hunter-gatherer way of life ... the San people have lived here for perhaps 30 000 years ... today there are between 1 000 and 2 000 people living permanently in the area ... the majority of these people live at Xade, a settlement in the reserve near the western border.'

But when we arrived at Xade – to which San communities had been moved over a period of 20 years – there were no San left at all. In some sleight of hand, the Botswana government had

created a settlement called New Xade, 70 kilometres away and 45 kilometres outside the reserve's western border, and moved everyone there. All that was left at Old Xade was a ranger's post, staff compound and campsite – nothing else.

Paul couldn't believe it. 'When we came through here in 1996 there was a huge settlement,' he exclaimed. 'They must have moved nearly 2 000 people.' The beehive huts with droopy roofs lay broken on the ground. At one destroyed settlement an enamel bucket and a paraffin tin, both valuable items, lay abandoned in the ruins of a kraal. The village had other pathetic signs of occupation and forced departure: thorn bushes dragged across the entrances of huts to keep out predators, the head of a plastic doll, a half-burned pile of fire sticks, a supermarket bag hanging in the thorns of a zizyphus.

At the game scout camp there was an air of military discipline. Some young guys playing soccer in the yard were on 'national service' with the Department of Wildlife and National Parks. In the office we were grilled: Why do we want to go to Xaxa and not Deception Pan? Why do we have a Basarwa (Bushman) with us? Are we really tourists? Why did we not book in at Gaborone the way we are supposed to? In the end the ranger relented, and gave us a pamphlet on the CKGR.

'The people commonly known throughout the world as Bushmen,' it says, 'but more properly referred to as the Basarwa, have been resident in and around the area for probably thousands of years. Originally nomadic hunters and gatherers, the lifestyle of the Basarwa has gradually changed with the times and they now live in settlements, some of which *were* [author's emphasis] situated within the southern half of the Central Kalahari Game Reserve. Government has, however, encouraged these people to move to areas outside the reserve in order that they may be provided with modern facilities, schools, clinics etc, and to integrate them into modern society.'

Government Notice number 38 of 1963 of the Bechuanaland Protectorate states that 'no person

other than a Bushman indigenous to the Central Kalahari Game Reserve shall enter the said reserve without having first obtained a permit in writing from the District Commissioner in Ghanzi.' But diamonds speak louder than moral rights in Botswana. The Kalahari desert is enormously rich in diamonds. They are already being extracted at Gope, another traditional home of the Basarwa, 36 kilometres inside the eastern section of the reserve. According to all the literature, the San have lived in the Central Kalahari for 30 000 years or longer – ergo, they own the land and the diamonds, the animals and the pans and the bushveld and the tourist revenue. That's how simple it is. And that's why the government cannot allow them to stay.

We set off for Molapo, about 200 kilometres and a hard day's driving away. After driving through fields of giraffe, kudu and bat-eared foxes, we arrived there in mid-afternoon when the light was beginning to turn golden. A small crowd gathered, all very young or very old. Slowly, carefully, younger men and women begin to emerge as the word spread that we were friends, not foe. They had been hanging back in case we were government and they needed to hide. We had found the bitter enders.

We cried as we listened to the stories, once because of their sadness, again because of their beauty. The chief of Molapo is Seqo G//anako. 'I was born here in Molapo,' he said, 'and my grandfather and his grandfather and his grandfather again are buried here under these trees. The government says we must move because of the wild animals, but my grandfather and his grandfather lived with the animals. They are like our goats; we have always had wild animals around us. We have always looked after them; we never killed more than we needed to eat. When I see wild animals all around us, my heart is happy: when I am hungry and I see them I think of food, but mostly when I see them they just make me very happy.'

At dusk we walked around Molapo with Custom Gabogalalwe, the chief's 29-year-old grandson. Custom's name is a 'protection' name, a Tswana name he has taken to disguise his origins in the face of Botswana's unofficial ethnic hierarchy.

'I think the government will come with guns, because we refuse to move from here to New Xade,' he said. 'I am not sure what we will do if that happens. This is our land; our traditional land. My great-great-grandfathers are buried here – how can we move? They say they want us out of here because of the animals, but we believe it is because of diamonds or oil. If they want to develop that, then they must talk to us; this is our land.'

Xowago Xam is a very old man with feet as tough as leather, and a famous hunter. 'Life here is very very good,' he said. 'There is veld food and bush medicine, and the animals are plentiful. They have always been like that, even in the long dry seasons. I will not move from here; I will die in this soil. If the government comes with guns and tries to move me, they can shoot me. I will not move; my blood will be in this soil.'

For years the village has been asking the government for a borehole, and for years it has been denied. Once a month the government sends a tanker with 10 000 litres of water for a settlement of 200 people – 50 litres of water per person, or less than two litres a day. Custom said they had been warned that if they fed any of the water to their livestock they would be arrested. His grandfather said: 'The game department has told us we have to move so that they can make a water hole here for the animals, so the tourists can come. And they don't want us near the animals.

'We get no money from the government for the tourists coming through here. We get tourists coming who want to go and walk in the bush, or see some dancing or buy some crafts, but the government tries to stop it. We want to work with tourists, and the government must understand that that is a good thing for this park.'

Like Xowago Xam, Chief Seqo Ga//nako is fatalistic: 'I think they will move in one day soon and order us out of here; they will come with guns and cars. If they come here with guns and lorries, we will just sit down. If the government wants to shoot us they can shoot us; we will not climb into their cars.'

Despite these pressures, Molapo remains a vibrant, buzzy community. In one corner a granny was skinning a mongoose for supper while her grandchildren crowded around. Across the fire, her daughter clipped ostrich shells, stringing the rounded bits on to a necklace. Next door a young boy herded goats into the kraal, and everywhere small fires started up at each clan's hut circle. The chief had given us a campsite within the village perimeter but outside the intimacy.

Custom and his friends came to visit after dark, and we shared a Kalahari stir-fry with mealie-meal porridge and relish. The talk turned to diamonds. 'We have seen the vehicles,' said one youth; 'some of them were marked "De Beers".' The young men were fired up with talk of resistance, and insisted they wanted to live in the bush and not in Ghanzi. 'If you are in town and you have got money,' joked Custom, 'you can go straight to the supermarket and be a hunter-gatherer there. But it is much better and much more pleasure to go and hunt and gather in the bush.'

That night the lions came to Molapo. I following their progress by the shouting, banging of pans and whistling that started at one end of the village and moved through to the other, via the dogs barking, donkeys braying and stoking of fires. Then I fell asleep.

The next morning we laboured out through the deep sand and did 180 kilometres in seven hours, reaching New Xade by late afternoon. This is the place to which the Bushmen of the Central Kalahari have been moved – their promised land.

It is a wasteland. Estimates are that 2 000 or more Bushmen have been relocated to New Xade. There is hardly a shrub in sight. The trees are all grazed to the height of a goat standing on its hind legs. Beer cans are the only spots of bright colour. Litter hangs in all the thorn trees, and plastic bags vibrate on the barbed wire fences. A drunken man demanded that Paul photograph him, and as we drove through the kids ran out screaming 'sweets, sweets'. There is an air of listlessness and despair, a feeling that this is the end of the road.

There are airconditioned bungalows with solar-heated showers and satellite TV for the government workers in their own compound. Everybody else lives in urban squalor. Many are still waiting for their compensation of five cattle, eight donkeys, 15 goats and ploughing implements. Some of the adults earn 80 pula a month (R100) on drought relief projects. We hear stories about prostitution rings run for the construction workers who are tarring the wilderness roads.

We found an ancient culture that was being destroyed in a war of attrition by thirst even as you read this story. New Xade is the prisoner of war camp. It has bad grazing, unfamiliar veld foods, and very little game. An old woman came in from the veld. She was carrying a pitiful bundle of fire sticks and roots. Her name was Xaojuswe Phela. I asked her: 'How is life here in New Xade?'

She hawked deep in her throat, and spat in the sand. There was blood in her phlegm. 'There is no life here, she said. 'I just sit like this and try and gather, but there is very little veld food, I don't know how I will live. I am lost now. They must just take me to the bush and bury me, because the government has thrown us away.'

'*Some people tell us that there is a black Government, we do not see it, we do not feel its presence, all we feel is the same old heat of threatened forced removals. Life is not good here. We are hounded, worse than wild animals. But all those who claim to love the environment but exclude black people, they must know that we will never leave this forest. They might as well kill us, keep us in their deep-freezers and feed us to their beloved crocodiles.*'

Baba Msele, Dukuduku forest, St Lucia, Maputaland (SA)

Uneasy paradise

A journey through Maputaland

By Victor Munnik and Gcina Mhlope

'My people, the Mbuyazi people, should never part with the sea. We are ocean people; when you remove us from the sea, it is the same as taking a fish out of the water. We die.'
Chief Phineas Mbuyazi

Maputaland, the northernmost part of the South African province of KwaZulu-Natal, is a place of great beauty, and its mountains, bushveld, lakes and coastal features have attracted people for a very long time. Stone implements found in the area show that people lived there from at least the Middle Stone Age onwards; iron smelting furnaces dating back to about AD 630 have been discovered. In the intervening period, forests were largely supplanted by secondary grasslands, which attracted zebra and impala and the carnivores which followed them in turn.

For the past 700 years, the inhabitants of Maputaland have tried to conserve its natural resources as part of their way of life. This has not been easy; the area's wealth has always attracted outsiders. Early in the 19th century the local Thonga people were incorporated into an expanding Zulu empire. Early European explorers were followed by hunters who slaughtered elephants for their ivory. In 1917 the anti-nagana campaign (nagana is a cattle disease then wrongly thought to be carried by wild animals) led to the indiscriminate killing of tens of thousands of head of game.

Even though these schemes failed commercially, the introduction of cotton, sugar and forestry in the second half of the 20th century led to the destruction of many hectares of bush. Next, a big dam was built on the Pongola River, disrupting the finely tuned local system of floodplain agriculture. And in the 1970s the apartheid government hatched a scheme to sell the northern half of Maputaland to Swaziland; the Swazis intended building a harbour at Kosi Bay which would have destroyed endangered turtle breeding grounds, the habitat of rare palm nut vultures, ancient fish kraals, and much more.

Ironically, the latest invaders have come in the name of saving the natural beauty of the area: they are conservation officials, or 'nature', as they are known locally. They have brought with them forced removals, bans on hunting and snaring, and limits on the traditional use of natural resources. However, after initially forming part of the European colonial invasion and later of the apartheid dispensation, conservation officials

have begun to change their approach; after all, in 1994 a democratically elected government took power. Thus communities living next to protected areas or claiming back land that was taken away from them have been involved in development projects, especially ecotourist projects. The nature of conservation, too, has been changing private conservation, and its commercial expression, tourism, has made major inroads on state conservation.

And Maputaland does have rich tourist resources. Stretching south of Mozambique, between Swaziland and the coast, the region encompasses six ecological zones starting with the Lebombo mountains in the west, followed by thornveld, sand forest, a mosi palm belt (the palms are used to brew a potent wine), a string of coastal lakes surrounded by wetlands, and the coast itself. Coral reefs flourish in the warm Indian Ocean. At the southernmost tip of

Maputaland lies Lake St Lucia, declared a world heritage site in 1999. It is the biggest and best known of the coastal lakes, and a paradise for tourists.

It is into this paradise – and this changing political situation – that the five of us – photographer Paul Weinberg, journalist Victor Munnik, storyteller Gcina Mhlope, filmmaker Carl Becker, and Mhlope's and Becker's four-year-old daughter Nomakwezi (star of the morning), venture in May 1999. Our journey starts off quite happily, but as we progress we increasingly encounter confusion, misunderstandings and conflict, leaving us with a growing sense of sadness and loss.

We start out at the Phinda Resource Reserve, an exclusive private game reserve at the northern end of Lake St Lucia. Its general manager, Les Carlisle, explains its approach to the communities

Who can claim the sea as theirs?

The sea is large, and full of happy rhythms. And tell me, who can claim it as theirs? Who can claim to have taught it those unpredictable and hypnotic rhythms?

And please tell me how large the Indian Ocean is – in square metres, yards, kilometres or hectares... I wonder if anyone can actually pretend to know. Maybe the Sun knows – he has roamed the skies for as long as the sea has been around; they know each other so well.

Both know too about the world's most unfathomable creation: people.

People are drawn to beautiful places, to hear lovely sounds, taste sweet fruit, smell flowers, and revel in all kinds of atmospheres presented to us by God the Creator. But then, why is it that humans are the ones who hurt nature most? Humans are also the ones who will fight and claim ownership of almost anything within their reach. I love stories; how I wish the Sea

and the Sun would call me for at least one month's session of storytelling. I bet the stories they'd share would be so magical all my senses would jump and move to all sorts of new rhythms.

Well, in May 1999 I came to St Lucia on the North Coast of KwaZulu-Natal. My first response was one of awe at the very beauty of the place. My heart longed to stay on; I even wished I could build a house and settle there – as close to the sea as possible, or at least within view of it. But then I was not on holiday; I had come with a team looking to meet people and talk about life and the current battles in the place.

What battles? Ownership, of course; what else? There are many stories, and many versions of the same stories, and too little time to hear them all. So we went and met some people, and heard some stories. The place looked really calm on the outside; the birds sang their ancient songs, not caring to stop and ask who we were and why we'd come.

around it: 'We aren't liberals with guilty conscience,' he notes. 'We do development work in our neighbouring communities as part of our business strategy. To conserve an island of biodiversity in a sea of poverty you have to deal with the poverty too; you have to mitigate the subversive potential of the neighbouring communities. So we focus on our three immediate neighbours.'

How? 'You have to ignite the local economies,' says Carlisle. This is the job of development officer Isaac Tembe, supported by the CCAfrica Foundation. Formerly the Rural Investment Fund, the foundation has been established by CCAfrica (formerly Conservation Corporation Africa), which owns and manages a series of private game reserves throughout Africa, Phinda among them. The role of the foundation is to develop communities adjacent to and on CCAfrica reserves.

From the comfort of our wooden deck we gaze out at giraffes grazing among the thorn trees below, and admire the opulent R1 500-a-night

chalets of burnished wood, glass, and thick thatch. A foundation pamphlet attracts our attention. It shows happy children at school, people working in a laboratory, a young woman who has just harvested *ncema* grass with which she will weave traditional mats, a sister bandaging a patient's arm. Then Tembe takes us out into the areas around the reserve to inspect the investments Phinda has made in the neighbouring communities.

The foundation has built a clinic in the Makasa tribal area nearby, with additional funding from the Independent Development Trust. Phinda has also built a home for expectant mothers at the clinic. The nursing staff is provided by the provincial government. But the general poverty of the area makes itself felt here as well. There are only four sisters − because the province cannot afford more − and they work 12-hour shifts around the clock, handling between 120 and 150 cases a day. These include deliveries, immunisations, minor illnesses, family planning,

and chronic patients such as diabetics and hypertensives. A doctor flies in every Thursday, and an ambulance is available for emergencies. Saturdays and Sundays, says a weary sister Molly Dlungwane, are taken up with doing paperwork and ordering supplies. On another front, 20 new classrooms have been added to schools at Makasa and in two other neighbouring communities, and libraries and laboratories established. So far, 32 bursaries for further studies have been awarded.

At the Makasa tribal authority office people declare that being Phinda's neighbours has brought good luck. Maps on the walls show the schools, clinic, and the marketplace that will be built next to the new tarred road which, as part of the Lubombo Spatial Initiative, will connect St Lucia with Ponto do Ouro in Mozambique. Tembe tells us that community leaders often call him or other Phinda personnel in for advice when dealing with powerful outside interests.

While travelling, Tembe tells us that he comes from Kosi Bay in the far north. He has been with Phinda for five years now. Before that he was employed by the University of Zululand as a development worker, specialising in appropriate and alternative technology such as rain water harvesting.

Tembe says the people of Kosi Bay still carry the baggage of their past struggles with provincial conservation officials; it seems to him that state conservation has done little to undo the damage of the past. He particularly remembers the trick state conservation officers played on the Kosi Bay communities when the latter asked for a low fence to be erected to protect them and their crops against hippos. The authorities used this as an excuse to erect a high fence around the communities and prohibit them from fishing and farming in the swamps.

This was done by the KwaZulu Bureau for Natural Resources (KBNR). A particularly hated body, the KBNR was the conservation arm of the 'homeland' of KwaZulu, established under the apartheid system. Conservation in the rest of Natal, remaining part of 'white' South Africa, was managed by the Natal Parks Board. Since South Africa's transition to democracy in 1994, these two bodies have been amalgamated into the KwaZulu-Natal Conservation Service.

Tembe's words takes me back to my first visit to Kosi Bay a number of years ago, when I saw the fence for myself. And I recall the local topic of conversation at the time, namely the strange belief of white people that they knew best how to conserve nature.

Then, my companions and I walked on the dunes between the Indian Ocean and the Kosi Bay lake system, where the famous fish kraals are. The sand was hot enough to scorch our feet. Fortunately we found trees laden with sweet purple berries. We eventually joined some people sitting on mats in the shade of a tree. One of them, an old man, had worked in Johannesburg for most of his life. He had been drinking palm wine all morning. When he called for a gun to shoot the hippo which kept damaging his field, an elderly woman waved her walking stick at him and cried: 'Keep quiet, you old fool!'

We shared our biscuits with them, and they offered us palm wine. For how long had they lived on the dunes? They smiled and said there was no one alive who could remember those who had first settled here. Then they complained about the newly erected fence: 'No one has explained

- 37 -

why it is there, and what it is really meant for. We are just told that they want to look after nature, and that we must not catch fish.'

I asked provocatively: 'So is it true that you don't look after nature?'

The palm wine drinker responded with a forceful epithet. But the woman, Elita Thembu, formulated a careful answer: 'Our forefathers and we have looked after nature, because we live from it. I look after the *umdoni* (berry trees) here; I prune them and make them produce more fruit. The problem is that outside people want to control nature for us.'

When I recount this story, Isaac Tembe responds with a knowing sigh: 'Those conservation officials were ignorant. They were intruding.' The question is, to what extent have they changed?

That night we move to a resort on the shores of Lake St Lucia; the lake forms part of the Greater St Lucia Wetland Park, run by the KZN Conservation Service. The sun set redly over the water, to the sounds of birdsong. It is hard to believe we are not in paradise. Personnel come to clean our cottage, and even offer to cook our food.

The next day we join tourists for a two-hour boat trip on the lake. One can buy coffee or tea, chocolate cake or muffins, or even a beer or spirits before ascending to the top deck where it is just you, the sun, the lake – and the voice of our guide, Promise Mdletshe. He explains everything

we notice, and a great deal we don't. First is a pied kingfisher, which nests in little holes in the banks of the lake. The little bird plunges into the muddy waters of the lake and emerges with a writhing fish. 'The fishing here is really good,' comments Mdletshe.

Lake St Lucia is the biggest inland body of water in South Africa, 40 kilometres long, with another 20 kilometres of narrows connecting it to the Indian Ocean. In the park, coastal, lake, wetland and savannah ecosystems combine to form a rich and diverse habitat for plants, birds and fish – a tourist's dream.

Mdletshe explains that the mangrove trees growing out of the mud on the shores have roots to help them breathe, and push out extra salt from the salt water through their leaves.
The mangroves host two amazing creatures: the mudskipper, a fish with two front legs which has learnt how to breathe out of the water, and the fiddler crab, which has one large nipper to attract females and one small one.

Reedbuck and vervet monkeys run through the dry forest which starts close to the shoreline.
A woman in the tour group stares out over the dunes on the eastern shore. She tells her companions: 'Do you know, Richard's Bay Minerals wanted to mine these dunes. Can you believe it, they said they would restore the dunes afterwards. That is impossible.'

'These are the highest vegetated dunes in the world,' Mdletshe booms. 'Look to your left; these are wild date palms. People make beer from the fruit. The leaves are used for crafts ...'

After disembarking, we visit a craft market near the landing stage where one can buy little 4x4 vehicles carved from wood, reed mats, baskets and so on, and cheaply too. It is even cheaper when you buy from the stalls along the road through Dukuduku forest before you enter the village of St Lucia.

There are also curios at the fresh fruit stalls in St Lucia itself. Resident journalist Niki Barker tells us that the little town has 450 permanent

residents, 'all of them white'. After our visit we read in newspapers that the white residents have tried – unsuccessfully – to put up a barrier boom and start a curfew at night.

St Lucia is a favourite destination of white fishermen from all over the country. They catch so much fish that they arrive with deep-freezes on their 4x4 vehicles.

Many of the black people who work in St Lucia live in the nearby Dukuduku forest, where they grow their own food – as well as pawpaws and bananas they sell to tourists – in clearings in the forest. Dukuduku is one of the very last coastal forest ecosystems left in South Africa, and both the national Department of Forestry and the provincial conservation service desperately want to conserve it – which means to them that the people now living in the forest should leave.

So the right to stay on the land is the main issue for people in the forest. There have been attempts at forced removals, protests, barricades on the road, threats against tourists… The government has negotiated with some groupings, bought them farms and tried to resettle them, but people have time and again returned to the forest, or newcomers have moved in.

With Barker as our guide, we venture into the forest. The paths and dirt roads are very confusing, and without her we would have driven around for many hours. No one would have led us to the people we are looking for; everyone here is suspicious of strangers.

The couple we have come to see have just returned home, so we are lucky to find them. They make us feel at home and tell us their story. They make us promise, though, that we won't use their real names – so we will call them Mkhize. They tell us that they weren't born in the forest, but have lived there for a long time. They really feel at home there, and wish to stay for the rest of their lives, and have made up their minds that they will resist any attempt to remove them. They live a simple but comfortable life.

Their homestead consists of several round huts, well-built and immaculately kept. They seem to know how to make the most of their environment. Besides their beauty, many of the indigenous flowers, plants and trees that surround the house are utilised for their medicinal or nutritional value. The refreshing drink we are offered comes from a wild fruit found here in abundance.

The couple tell us that the forest community has been so troubled by the possible forced removal that relations have become strained; people have begun accusing one another of selling out to the authorities. There is tension and suspicion, and yet so much love for this place. 'You see, this forest is very fertile,' says Mrs Mkhize. 'It has good soil for us to grow our vegetables and mealies, which is our staple food. The pawpaws and other fruit are sweet and nourishing. The forest is like a blanket, giving us comfort and solace. Why would we want to leave such a home behind?'

Mkhize adds: 'People are getting angry with me because they don't see why I should be prepared to talk to the white people. I am not selling out; I only want our side of the story to be heard too. I just hate the idea that we should boycott the meetings called by the authorities at the expense of being misunderstood and misrepresented.

'The people of this community have been living such uncertain lives. The news comes that we will definitely have to go. Weeks later everyone hears the rumours that we are not going after all; some agreement has been reached, and Kader Asmal [the then national minister of forestry] and his people have decided it's better that we stay. What a relief! We sleep better again, but before long we hear the opposite. Now what are we to believe?

'Those of us who don't want to leave this place are very prepared to co-operate with the authorities in their plans to save it. But why do they have to chase us out? We certainly care more about it than anyone else. I remember

several meetings when we asked them to teach us whatever special knowledge they have to make this a safe heritage site. We are willing to learn new things to add to what we already know. Why hire outside people to care for this place? We, the community of Dukuduku forest, want to do that. You know, there are so many contradictions here – they love the trees, the birds and the animals, but they want us out! In their minds we are not part of the nature of this place.'

The forest could be conserved by the people living there already, Mkhize argues; then they could run tourists businesses inside the forest. All this would be possible, if only the KZN Conservation Service could make friends with the community in the forest. 'But now the service has told its community officer not to deal with the forest people until things have been settled.

'We have been told in no uncertain terms that we will never have electricity, a clinic, or piped water as long as we stay in the forest,' Mkhize

adds. And then he gives us a glimpse of his dream: 'I have cleared a site here for an ecotourist hut and a restaurant. From these windows I and my guests, when they come one day, will be able to see the sea.'

We drive past the Mzabalazo Primary School, established in 1995. These children carry their desks out of the one-roofed room every morning and carry them back at the end of the school day. Their classes are held under trees. When it rains, they go home for the day. There are 313 children in seven classes, five teachers, and one principal. Three are paid by the state, and two by the community. Some parents cannot afford the R75 per child a year, but their children are still at school. 'What can you do?' sighs the teacher talking to us; 'their parents are not working.'

'We have borrowed books from other schools – but this is a real school, recognised by the government. The fact is, the government has no money,' says teacher Ntombifuthi Mhlanga. She says she is against people being chased out of the forest, as much as she is against people chopping down trees and hurting the environment. 'The children's parents grow food and sell bananas and mangoes. They do not have enough. Often the children come to school hungry.'

The Mkhizes have been members of the school committee since its inception, and have worked very hard to create a functioning school; it is still in the process of being established. In the meantime, the classes are held under the trees.

A blackboard leans against a tree trunk, and the teacher stands in front of several rows of desks. The pupils are neatly dressed and hungry for knowledge. It all looks pretty romantic, until rain clouds gather and heavy drops dictate that the school day is over. There is nowhere to hide, for either the teachers or pupils – they are equally vulnerable to cold winter winds, rain, and hot summer sun. But the will to teach and learn keeps them going while they wait for their school to be built and for the future of their forest to be decided.

Luckily, they can still learn about the history of the forest they call home from older people – such as Baba Joconia Msweli – who have been there for a long time.

And this is where the Mkhizes take us next – to the home of Baba Msweli, on the edge of the forest. He welcomes our interest in Dukuduku's history, and talks fluently about his ancestors – a long line of chiefs and indunas, who came to the forest several generations ago. His grandfather, Mkhalakathana Msweli, was a respected chief who was elected by King Shaka Zulu himself to rule the area; 'you see, we Msweli people are closely related to the royal Mthethwa people, who brought up King Shaka from an early age'.

Msweli is an induna, as was his father before him. How, we ask, did Mineus Mkhwanazi, the current chief resident at Mtubatuba, come into the picture?

'Chief Mkhwanazi arrived here from Swaziland. He found all the Msweli chiefs and went behind our backs to the royal place. He asked for a royal widow's hand in marriage, and they agreed.

'He married Ntikili the widow, then he wriggled his way back here and into power – *wayeshuka izikhakha*. The then ruling king gave him superior powers over the Mswelis. That is how Mkhwanazi became chief here, and we were made *abanumzana* and *indunas*. But there is no hatred between us; we will always respect a person's position.

'Recent chaos here has made people speculate that maybe we Mswelis want to take over the power of the chief. That is not so; we want to work together. All we are really fighting for is the land and the forest. The current chief has been heard to say: "I know nothing; I'm young, let those who know speak up."

'Well, here we are. We will speak up about the whole history of this land. We know too that the great king Goodwill Zwelithini [the present Zulu monarch] will be pulled into this battle. He knows, just as we do, that we are not trespassing here, that this place is rightfully ours. The white people who now want to throw us out found us here. They pretended that they wanted to live with us, but then they started buying huge chunks of our land from each other. We are not talking money here; the value of this place cannot be measured in money. They must stop promising us little amounts of money and think that will satisfy us and make us happy about leaving the bones of our ancestors.

'If anyone at all has to go from here, it is these horrible trees – the pines, jacarandas and gum trees. They are not good for our soil; we don't want them here; even their leaves look like the hair of white people. The local trees are like us; the leaves resemble my curly hair. These trees have belonged to this place from the beginning of time; we identify with them, we call them *Velekhona*, which means "always here". Do you see that big one over there? Underneath it is the grave of my mother.

'And the grass hut you see here, it is the place where I was born, and my children too, a place my ancestors find it easy to enter when they visit us. It is where we perform ancestral ceremonies. The thatch grass is also unique in that it keeps us warm in winter and cool in summer, and protects us from wind and rain. I feel very proud about our way of life. We will not allow the authorities to throw us out of here; what gives them the right to do that?

'I have worked for the Parks Board as a guard on several of its game reserves, and I'll tell you this: those people are so two-faced! I've been to Kings Park, Mhlali, Shakaspruit, Mvoti, Nseleni, St. Lucia, Sodwana, Bhangasi and Khiwathi. In those years I have learnt that, to these people, all this talk of preserving nature is mostly a way of running a business. They make money, and pay us as little as possible. They shoot the animals whenever they wish, and we have no way of questioning them. They write the books, they read them, and then tell us that the knowledge in those books is the one and only truth – just because it's written down. But who wrote those books?

They themselves! What would they say if my son wrote a book and went around telling them that all that is written in that book is good and perfect? They'd say he was mad.

'I believe in the preservation of this place. There is no tree, bird or animal I do not know here. Dududuku is life to me. I love many of these animals like I love my father's cattle. We hunted animals and enjoyed their meat, but we had specific times to do that and we gave them time to breed and multiply. These strangers treat us like mindless little people. We have all our senses and knowledge of this place. Without the care we feel for this forest, it would have been destroyed long ago. They are the ones who brought strange trees and bushes that are strangling the local trees, in the same way as their tourism ideas are strangling the very life out of us.

'It is all so ironic how they can calmly say one thing today and then do another tomorrow. In many parts of KwaZulu-Natal white people have destroyed communities, chased people away, planted large parts with sugar cane, foreign woodlands, and put up factories that leak oil into

the rivers without caring about nature or the people. They think we are stupid and we do not see that. You know, in the times I worked for them, we used to be told to shoot an old hippo, cut it to pieces and serve it to the crocodiles. They knew we also like the meat, but no, they would not give us a piece to eat with our families. As far as they are concerned we are not part of this nature they are so in love with; we the indigenous people of this land are not part of this environment, we are not needed. Why is it that they cannot respect our ways of life and doing things? Yet they expect us to respect theirs. It drives me mad to know that they shoot wild animals as they please and sell the meat in their expensive restaurants without any bad conscience.

'Some people tell us there is a black government. But we do not see it, we do not feel its presence; all we feel is the same old heat of threatened forced removals. Life is not good here. We are hounded, worse than wild animals. But all those who claim to love the environment but exclude black people, they must know that we will never leave this forest. They might as well kill us, keep us in their deep-freezes, and feed us to their beloved crocodiles.'

Baba Msweli laughs: 'And the way these people don't care for us, I wouldn't put it past them! But I promise them that my people will fight to the end. Those few who have been bribed and wish to go, they are free to do so, we won't stop them. We are like the indigenous trees of Dukuduku; we cannot go, we belong here.'

After our visit to the forest, the conflict flares up again. This time it centres on the annual harvesting of *ncema* – a type of sedge used for making mats which form part of traditional bride wealth. The *ncema* stand is one of only two left in KwaZulu-Natal, and is jealously guarded by conservation officials who assess annually how much can be sustainably harvested by local people. The harvesters – mostly women – pay R3 each for a permit to cover the conservation service's administration costs.

This year, on the weekend before the harvest, Dukuduku rebel Timothy Mphanga's supporters stage a demonstration on the main route to St Lucia, claiming that the land between Dukuduku and St Lucia, including the *ncema* stand, belongs to them. We cannot get hold of Mphanga, and hear the story from conservation service officers. They say the Mphanga group insists the harvesters must pay it R10 each. The conservation service tries to negotiate, but three days later police and protesters are firing at each other – the police with rubber bullets and teargas, the protesters with AK47 assault rifles. Finally the protesters go home and the harvesting goes ahead under protection of the South African Police Service, which builds temporary shelters for the harvesters outside the forest.

Mphanga's group is part of a complex problem for the national Department of Forestry, which has bought two nearby sugar farms for relocating the forest dwellers. The problem is that the different groups in the forest – people with ancient land claims, people who have moved in recently, people who have already moved out, and people who are accused of gun running and being illegal immigrants – have different interests, and are not all willing to negotiate with the government.

The conservation service treats the people who have already moved out of the forest as a 'neighbouring community', involving them in development (electricity, water and other infrastructure) as well as ecotourism projects. They now live just outside the forest to the north of the tarred road.

After our visit to Dukuduku we are depressed, confused and angry. These feelings turn into a deep sadness as we spend the last day of our journey with Chief Phineas Mbuyazi, who is living in fear of his life elsewhere in KwaZulu-Natal after filing a claim on behalf of his people for the eastern shores of St Lucia – the land between the lake and the sea. This has brought him in conflict with the powerful and feared chief Mineus Mkhwanazi, who has claimed the same piece of land.

It is not easy to find Mbuyazi. The roads are untarred and confusing. In a nearby town where we ask for directions, people are very protective of him and question our motives closely. But we do eventually find the chief, in the middle of a desolate plain, in a humble dwelling where he practises as a traditional healer.

He remembers some of us from earlier interviews, and shares the story of his life in exile with us: 'This is the place where I have been living for the past few years,' he says. 'I was forced to come here; I left my home because my life was under threat. I still don't feel safe.

'Originally I am from Bhangasi, at St Lucia by the sea. That is where I belong, and that is where all my ancestral history lies. That forest, Enkosini, is where we performed ancestral ceremonies year after year.

'My people, the Mbuyazi people, are ocean people – we should never part with the sea. When you remove us from the sea, it is the same as taking a fish out of water. My beloved wife of many years came here, and she could not take it. There is her grave, as you can see. It pains me to live without her. So I lost the sea and my wife.

'It hurts so very much; you can see how thin I am. I feel so out of place, so disconnected. I feel I could die any time too. To us the sea is life itself. It is as if a large part of my spirit has been amputated. I am like the shadow of the man I used to be. My heart bleeds for my children. All the time I worry and fear that if I die here in this strange kind of exile, they will have no sense of belonging. Our family name and ancestry will become meaningless.

'There is an animal – the hippopotamus – that is very much like a family totem, or a part of our family. It is sacred. We have always respected this animal. My father is the one who brought the first two hippos to the Bhangasi River. There always had to be hippo wherever our family lived because of the spiritual connection. Hippos are like brothers and sisters to me, and I do not want them hurt in any way. When I go to perform ancestral ceremonies in Bhangasi, I first go down to the river to talk to them and keep them in touch with the family. I can communicate with them, and they recognise my spirit.

'When we were growing up we were taught two important things: to respect animals, and to respect the trees and plants that are all around us. Our parents and grandparents taught us that we could not survive without them, so we must always take good care and think about what we did.

'As the hippo is sacred to my family, the leopard is sacred to our [Zulu] nation. We very rarely hunted a leopard, and then it was only for the king's royal robe. The young men who were sent out to hunt one were given express orders not to stab it but to hit it with a club or stick. The young man who succeeded in bringing back the king's robe would be rewarded with a cow.

'The skin of the *insimango*, a species of monkey, was also part of the king's attire. We were allowed to kill only four, and only after three years would orders be given for them to be hunted again. The rest of the time the animals were free to roam around, and to multiply happily. All other kinds of hunting were controlled, and nobody ever went hunting when it was not the season. People respected those rules. It was the same with harvesting the crops from the fields. We first had what we call *ukweshwama*, the taste of the first fruit by the king.

'We also loved wild fruit such as *umdoni* and *umnwebe*. People enjoyed carving wood, but we were taught from an early age that we should not

cut trees randomly. We had to look where the tree was located, and how old it was. Maybe it had medicinal powers too, so we had to take good care. I am one of those people who respect the soil as my own mother; it cannot be bought or sold. Now our people are being bribed with a bit of money, and they are expected to happily move away from their heritage. Anyway, money does not last, but the land is always there – to give us a home, food, water, heritage, and a sense of belonging. Also, land should be shared with others – I dislike any form of selfishness.

'With regard to the problem we have at Dukuduku and St Lucia – there are so many interested parties. Power and control is still at the centre of it all. I've often said that to us displaced people freedom is not here yet – we only hear people talking about it. Many of us feel as if the old regime has never left. And you can be sure I do not say this just because I hate the Parks Board. I so wish that they would be willing to respect our own local authorities and ways of life. Somehow there has to be a way of coming together and working together on this problem. I wish for us all to be united, for us to learn from one another. I wish they could be humble enough to see that there are things they can learn from us about the land of our birth – a land whose balanced wellbeing means so much to us.

'I am sorry that so few people out there know about our open-minded stance. If we can win back our land, our people would be so happy; I would be close to the sea again; my soul would be at peace. I would rebury my wife. And, best of all, we would happily welcome tourists and other visitors to our beautiful country. We have always been warm and friendly to strangers. And I know the hippos would also rejoice with us.'

Mbuyazi's land claim has since been settled; however, it came in the form of money instead of a return to the land, and he still lives in exile.

'All the way to here
it means here is something
I have something which you do not have
and you have something which I do not have
and thus we find unity
because the days of "baas" are past and gone'

Oom Jan, Richtersveld (SA)

It takes a lot of God to survive here

The Richtersveld National Park

By Antjie Krog

The Richtersveld National Park – a mountain desert park in Namaqualand, South Africa's arid north west region – is regarded as one of the few success stories in the history of parks and communities in Africa. As the first contractual national park in the country, no land was expropriated and no communities moved to establish it. Therefore, former inhabitants do not hang around at the park's entrances in desperate attempts to benefit from an industry controlled by outsiders. Instead, in establishing the park the South African National Parks Board has taken a different route.

The board rents the land from its original inhabitants, while allowing them to continue their stock farming. What makes the park even more unique is the fact that a private mining company is also paying local communities directly for diamond mining rights in the park. It means that, in an area of 162 445 hectares, stock farmers can graze their goats, Transhex mine diamonds, and tourists visit the park.

The park was established in 1991 in one of seven rural districts in Namaqualand. These rural areas for 'coloured' people were originally populated in the 17th century when white and black latecomers to the Cape forced its indigenous brown people to flee to outlying areas for survival, and missions stations were established there. In 1963 these stretches of land were officially classified as 'coloured' reserves under apartheid legislation.

The Richtersveld is one of South Africa's poorest regions. Yet, after Gauteng, it has the second richest mineral deposits, which are being mined but without any real return to the community. The moment a deposit was discovered, the land was summarily taken away from the local people. No wonder that land ownership is a controversial issue here – the first land claims were lodged in the 19th century, and others continue to this day. In one current claim, inhabitants are claiming back land from the state mine Alexkor on which their forefathers are buried.

Conversations with people in the Richtersveld reveal that they are generally well informed about the park's value, its advantages for the community, as well as the obligations it imposes on them. However, despite good co-operation between the inhabitants, the parks board and the mines, it is difficult to maintain a balance between tourism, mining, protected species, and farmers and their stock, and problems arise which require continual attention.

The mines have made certain areas inaccessible to as well as dangerous for livestock and people, and also consume huge quantities of water. Unsightly areas have been created. Although Transhex has promised to rehabilitate the land, it is not possible to do so everywhere. Mining also diminishes the experience of a remote wilderness area, because mining vehicles create high levels of noise and dust. The stock farmers find it very difficult to stick to their stock quotas; as a result, overgrazing is destroying some of the area's famous endemic biodiversity. All the farmers have dogs, which prey on the smaller animals. Some livestock graze at the campsites and spread parasites. In turn, the farmers complain about the mess left behind by tourists.

So, in the Richtersveld, everyone has his own narrative: whether landscape or human.

1. Narrative of the Big Gariep

the poles were not frozen –
the sea a slow gigantic circling gyre of lukewarm
water around Gondwanaland

until the breakup
then this continent softly wiggled herself loose
from the others
seeing how they drifted away as horizons

this was the birth of the Great River
the primordial Orange
'we don't call him Gariep,' says Oom Jakobus de Wet
'we call him Orange
but actually for us he is: The River'

separate from the others southern Africa shoots up from the sea
fluttering with looselimbed eustatic liberation
lakes and seas draining the tilting landscape
flattening   eroding
the primordial river scrambles over bedrock
through ducts   truncates granite
picks up speed   foams past the Gloryhole faultline
and rows towards the sea at last
with siltsoft velvet sediments slipping on to river banks

'the main thing about the Richtersveld is the mist,'
claims Dawid Links of the Parks Board
'it is him whom we Namas call: Huries
he wells up from the cold troughs of the Benguela
blown on land by wind, then limps across the veld
here the kopjes intercept it
so you know: bushes, stones – they all now drink dew
too much Huries, the old people said, makes the veld blue
the best for us here is land weather – for more fluent watering.'

   Dwyka ice is a name in my language
and granite of the Vioolsdrif suite!

the snake
(shhh! You musn't mention his name,
he will figure out exactly who you are)
he of the Great River, if he has had you and held you
he never lets go of you
you always always have to come back
the same time the same place every year
you will penetrate back always to the river
you can resist or rise above
but back you will always come back
like the woman
whether she bakes bread
whether she sits in church
when she hears him whistling
she gets up and walks
like a sleepwalker
back back to the river

he has a terrible power when he takes you
like compulsion   like a dream
afterwards you remember nothing
only the diamond on his forehead
and that he comes out at night to graze
putting the diamond aside on the grass
you can steal his power if you put wet cowdung over the diamond
and run away without trace
some people say he lives in the Wonderhole these days
of which nobody has fathomed the depth
only the illiterate man from Kubus
who went down and even deeper down
when he surfaced his hair was cloudwhite
and his voice gone
until his death no one knew what he had seen

2. Narrative of old nomadic movement patterns

In winter the people from Paulshoek trek to
Moedverloor, Boggel, Goeiemanskuil, Slootjies,
Damme, Een Wilger en Kuile. Rooifontein's
people set up camp at Matjiesgoedkloof,
Kammassies, Dikkopskraal and Draai. From Klein
Nourivier the trek road runs through Besitwater,
Khiribes, Bobbejaanshoek, Hosabes en Rooihoog.
Depending on the rain, Spoegrivier treks to
Skêrberg, Koringhoog and Patrysvlei. Klipfontein
treks to Nuwekloof, Vaaldraai, Gowermentsputs.
Tweerivier to Golfkraal and Haasrivier.
Oom Jakobus treks from Ochta to Pokkiespram,
and later to Oena. Ploegberg. Grootderm.
Windwaai. Kabies.

'This pattern was completely overturned by the
establishment of economic units.'
Land Use in Namaqualand, by Henry Krohne
and Lala Steyn

3. Narrative outside the park

Maria Johanna Domroch of Kubus
'Grandpapa Mandela for him I voted
why is it that to be a Nama today means something?
why do you come all the way to Kubus?
why am I on television?
because we are now somebody
under the old government we were nothing
over years we have been driven out to the most barren of places
Coloured Reserves
we were nothing
but today we are something
and it is him, that old man Mandela, it's him
no, Mandela and them got my vote'

the church in Kubus stands white against the quartzite sky
the ridge blushing with voice
oh God blow and bleed your love on us
says Oom Adam
hand on the heart the congregation sings
ja Jeeesus is the rock
in a thirr-sty land
in a thirr-sty land
in a thirr-sty land
Thou art like vapour on me
Jeesus Jeeee-sus
Kubus *hangs* on the ridges of Rosyntjieberg

it takes a lot of God to survive here

Org Farmer of Eksteenfontein
'the name of the Bosluis Basters (bush-tick bastards)
is really the Bo-sluis Basters (upper-sluice bastards)
but never mind, let me get to the heart of the story
we were without haven, without school, without church
we moved out of nothing to here, to Eksteenfontein
naked it was naked from the top
there was no living soul
only one brown horse at the fountain
but for the rest there was nothing
but we spread here and multiplied here
I had to leave my family
while my body was a driver in Hondeklipbaai
and look at us today

today Eksteenfontein has the title of a town
we provide electricity we provide water
we have built it all'

Mrs Farmer of Eksteenfontein
'I am very close to cattle
a house is nothing to me
but the open veld
I grew up in the open veld
in a round little house
when we arrived here it was raining
and the daisies were so high
that when I squatted I was sitting under a floor of flowers
from that day I adopted this place
and love it until now
for the disposition
for the veld
the man-of-the-park fetched us one day
to show us the park where our cattle once grazed
but there was a puffadder in the road and the man stopped
drive over that thing, kill it, I shouted, it only wants to poison us
no, said the parksman and waited patiently for the snakething
to cross the road
he showed us the halfhuman
but really, that I am used to
but my eyes stabbed this way and that
for that bulb that we used to eat in the veld
it had such funny fingers
and myself and Kowa's mouth were watering
Kowa even took a knife to clean off the thorns
and so we walked and searched while the others were at the halfhuman
here I found it! the !Xona and I tore off a piece
but the man said you may not simply take a piece
and I told the man
what shall we do we have eaten this since a long time
then he said it should be protected for your children
then I said but our children do not eat bulbs
then he said myself and Kowa may each take one
Kowa silently pocketed another small one
but I am at peace now
I know they still grow somewhere'

4. Narrative of the diamond sorter

when my eyes look they see stone
we empty the gravel bin
and scrape unfolding little fans of stone with the gravel knives
and you look and you see it
and your whole body says: diamond
I am Jan Links from Kommagas
I am 42 years old
I have worked on the mines from the age of 16
I can work everything: the stripping machine cat 400
cat 769 with the hollow step everything
mine money is tough money
but mining is my blood
though I long for my wife and children every day

you remove the dead earth until you get diamond gravel
then, yes, then you see now you have arrived
a bit of life is emerging
the gravel starts shooting on the conveyor belt
the X-rays pick it up – weight, intensity
and it falls through the flaps into the bins
then we know

here I came to see it for the first time
an alluvial diamond – so rare its shine
its form as if someone has worked on it
even if it's brown or green or pink
you feel the shine blinding your body
about the small ones you have doubts
the big ones you just know
you may never pick up a diamond by hand
you lift it with a tweezer from the waterstones and river stone
you put it aside for counting and locking up.
Smuggle? Maybe at other mines, but not here in the Richtersveld, never

Of course one can smuggle, says Kiewiet Cloete of Kubus
one can smuggle niii-cely
if your nerves can take it
if your nerves will hold
because if you steal you steal from the sorting table
you cough, you stumble slightly over the gravel on the table
the glue on the side of your hand picks up the diamond
and you and everybody watch things from the white of their eyecones
security, the men with you, everybody knows something has happened
but not precisely what
because you have to be bloody quick
and that you smuggle out
through the X-rays which just pick up every second or third man
you must pick up the rhythm
or doves fly them out to Kubus
or two of you tie buck hooves to your feet
and walk to the wires where two other wait on hooves
and so you swop, you swop

Geologist to Paul Kruger in 1886:
'Mr President, the conglomerate gold beds and
enclosing sandstones and quartzites were sea-shore
deposits formed during the subsidence of a coastline in …'
Kruger to his wife: 'Mama, meet the gentleman who
was there when God made the earth.'
Thomas Pakenham, A History of the Boer War
(1993).

5. Narrative of stone

a landscape like this scares me
already between Brandkaros and Bloeddrif it begins to stone you
'here! I am stone' it says
'stone only stone
in its ugliest stoniest stone
yeah take it! I am fuckingrockbluntugly
I cast the first stone to bloodywell trash your notion of mountain or rock
or rock or God
to survive against me you need
   God and Jesus and a helluva lot of holy soul
or booze
a terrifying amount of booze
because daily I hurl you away over mountains
or scorch you thin and godblack in this desert of stone'

I step back on to the Parks Board verandah
stone is unforgeable I read
      insoluble
      inaccessible
give me language for stone I plead
after a day of crying in this wilderness of cliffs and stone
I want language
such as: the shimmering white bite of stone
such as: stone waterfall tumbling shard
how snug the collar of lichen and quartzite lard
of the flaming cockscomb of stone
I have become the bard

'it bloodywell rhymes!
I'm something, do you hear me you!
look me in the eyes and face me
I'm something
I weather brutally
   into stone shards against barren slopes
   filthy messy stonebloodyflakes
no cute stonewords will you bleed from me
no chopping or hijacking of me, stone, into language
I from here
prank past your traps of torn stone or tumbled stone
vomit of lines carrying molten stone leaking stone lashing stone
I taunt the stonelovingness of stroke stone
the turdsoft usefulness of grinding stone brey stone washing stone
I shit stone hard on your sudden budding stone heart

I am my own thing
I weather brutally
In my stony world I am stoned'

it is really ugly here, I think to myself
on the map I see we are
at the last tender bight before the Orange bleeds into sea
the river lifts its elbow
and tucks the Richtersveld softly into its inner arm

you are standing now at the most beautiful spot in the Richtersveld
his voice takes the shoes from my feet
he shows me plumes of magma
and elephantskin weathering on dolomite
I trace dolorite squirting like dark toothpaste through the crust of earth
lighter granite peeling off in regular layers
it breathes of faultline and matrixes of mud
there are three basic kinds of stone he says
that which has coagulate like ironstone and granite
those which were sedimented like sandstone, scale en mudstone
and those which were tranformed into marble and quarzite

that evening
for the first time
the obtuse hills
ladled light past the tabee tree

6. Narrative of a farmer in the park

Oom Jakobus de Wet speaks poetry

'around Jerusalem are mountains
here alone with the goats in the veld
are also mountains
but all around is God
the whole evening I feel Him coming from this side of Lizard Valley

the beginning of me
was at Tattasberg mountain which they now call Richtersveld
herding goats   the jackal gorge from the buttock to the stomach
the baboon is different he doesn't catch, he takes
he tears open at the hips
in order to thread the entrails
initially it was the mines which wanted land
then I asked: how can two men manage one woman?
Then they answered: oom Jakobus you manage upper ground
                              we manage under ground
so that was clear
their only law
is that there should be no goats where the planes want to land

then there was the man of the parks
Dr Robberts pleaded a week long for consent
old tears he cried ancient tears
but we say it is our land
the law has given it to us
why should another man manage our land?
I asked again: how can two men have one wife?
Who manages the wife?
Then they answer: partners – we will be partners
then we say we don't even know about park
never mind about partners
then they said the most beautiful places in the country
are becoming parks
and the Richtersveld is a beautiful place
it should stay for our children
now that we understood

but it is only the farmers in the park who have the plenitude of the park
the goats are my bank
they come from Kimberley to count the goats
and they come any time to check on overgrazing
then I have to sell
my grandchild Benjamin does the herding
his mouth told this to me this morning
himself he said he wanted to be a goatherd
and I am satisfied
God put into everybody his own talent
at night at the camp we needn't talk
we know where grazing took place and where it should take place
it is a good life to give to a child
every child has his honour
let me say it
it is tasty to be with a grandchild
he makes me laugh
he let me say improper things
it is good to be with him

because day and night one is alone here at the post with Christ
we talk
you can lie back
and look at Him with clear eyes
you only have to look
because spirit is always aware of spirit

Key agreements
There are three agreements surrounding the Richtersveld National Park:

1. Between the inhabitants of the Richtersveld and the South African Parks Board

The state rents the park from the inhabitants at 50 cents a hectare. The money goes into the Richtersveld Community Trust Fund, run by a council of four parks boards and five community representatives. Among other things, the money is used to fund two extra teachers at every school in the area, pay the transport costs of children attending high school in far-off towns, educational bursaries, and the training of field guides. The council members do not benefit directly from the fund, and most local people are reasonably satisfied with the way in which it is being run. The park is also committed to employing people from the region.
In return, the parks board manages the park in collaboration with farmers running stock in the park. However, just how much the board has done to develop the park is not always clear; no attempt has been made to provide basic facilities at sensitive campsites along the river, with the result that visitors camp anywhere and the banks are littered with toilet paper and other rubbish. It is also absurdly easy to enter the park without a permit or payment, and without anyone being aware of the illegal entrant's presence.
Although brochures flaunt the fact that there are more than 500 rare plant species in the park – including the biggest range of succulents in the world – no visual information or map is on offer at the information centre. There is also no geological information. No management plan has yet been drawn up by the board and inhabitants.

2. Between inhabitants of Namaqualand and Transhex mine

Transhex pays 5 per cent of its turnover into the Namaqualand Fund Trust, and the money is spread evenly over the whole region. 'Diamonds do not grow,' say local people, and the idea is therefore to create industries which will take over from the mines as they are worked out over the next decade. Each of the former 'coloured' reserves receive R350 000 a year. The trustees are community representatives. Planning is apparently constantly undermined by quarrels and favouritism. However, water and electricity have been brought to smaller villages, and community halls have been built. The next project is to provide mortuaries.

3. Between the parks board and Transhex

The parks board ensures that the mine restricts its activities to delimited areas, and that the land is rehabilitated. The mine provides infrastructure in the form of roads, transport, housing, sports and other facilities. There is a very cozy relationship between the parks board and the mine.

Alexkor's role unclear

Another state-run mine, Alexkor, is supposed to pay 30 per cent of its profits into the Alexkor Development Trust. But according to the mine it makes no profit, and the fund is therefore dormant. In the meantime, the community has lodged land claims against the mine and hopes to negotiate a new kind of contract with it. According to Transform worker Floors Strauss, the mine has deliberately slowed down the land claims while 'continuing to take out diamonds at great speed'. Richtersveld community leaders are bitter because the new government seems just as unwilling to meet their demands as the previous one was.

my goats are branded: swallowtail and half moon in front
        tri-square and swallowtail at the other ear
government has given me stud ram
a carcassholding ram a real praise goat
among my goats I can never do apartheid
my goats are one
then the blessing of the Lord is there
but if I divide
I will bring my end

all the way to here
it means here is something
I have something which you do not have
and you have something which I do not have
and thus we find unity
because the days of "baas" are past and gone'

over midday the heat sets firmly in the hills
stones are bleached into blue
at the camp between ebony and karee
Oom Jakobus turns the colon upside down
and spreads kidney fat like breath over the branches
the pinch of shade is so shallow he mutters next to the slaughtered orrogoat
on the radio on a tin
Cobus Bester reads the one o'clock news
I walk behind Benjamin Cloete as he takes his goats to the veld
lightfooted flightfooted he covers the dunes
haii-haii whistles his whip
the goats sink into the overgrown riverbanks
young river reed thorntree raisintree
they munch themselves into silence
Benjamin filters softly into a river willow shade
and now? I ask
'Ma'am can now catch a little slumber'

fragile lies the river
open artery in the heat
the landscape unthinkable without this browngreen cut
undestructibly older than the oldest human breath on stone
it feeds the goats of dream and the goats of dying
of nothing too many
of nothing too utterly few

the mountain on the other side looks as if it's leaking
against the midday hour the mountain slakes in blue
strain away in tainted bronze

the first vygies hiss in cyanide
when the sun looks out I am there   I am there in lavender blue

I look at my watch
it is twenty minutes to three
and it means nothing absolutely nothing
we drowse between shade and grazing and heat

the sun slopes down at last
the ridges echo of bleating as the big goats turn homewards
the strapped lambs fight with the riempies
nothing as soft as lambkin of goat
nothing as snouty
as delicately mouthed   defencelessly eyed
as lambkin of goat in the evening when dusks sets in
some get teat some foreign teat
and it's big bleat to flat bleat to smallforlorn bleat
to gay bleat to moan bleat to spoilt bleat
to the vexed bleat of boss bleat

the velvet of a goat lambkin's ear
slips through my palm
'how do I follow the lines towards you love
when the late light knells along the stones
how do I remember my shivering body in your hand
while you nibble down my spine
how do I grow you here love
next to the great river
so that the past brackish bitter year
can be sedimented into love?'

the goats come home
short woollen waterfalls plunge from the trees
    in the late noon dust
lambs and kraal and goat beards
flickering piss and square droppings
like the diamonds it also has form here
two nipples   callous knees
whatever they've eaten let them fart tonight
little horns like horny wings
which could be pure angel
but the transparent striped eyes of a male goat
speaks of the devil complaining to Satan, says Kiewiet
and outside Joseph is preaching
over there on the hill he stands swinging his arms
his voice blown in texts down to us

Joseph preaches for the stones the valleys
to the river he sings
to the goats the night he preaches
this child is an embarrassment on me grumbles oom Jakobus

colour never comes alone she says
colour never comes alone
at dusk the ridges become loose and fall away in soft blue frills
the pleated mountains turn into fire
into dramatic amber
the river is hushed into reflected floats of amber jelly
feel time and bird time set in
with the violence of colour and reed
a heron flies quietly down the valley
small birds chirp in tussles on the grass next to my tent
the mountain buries his stone in the water
amber and gold and red drift up from the night shades
there is a shiver of stone and river willows and reed
a dove on the cliff falls into sound

the sky becomes shell
behind the night darkness the mountains have cut the sun
it bleeds through the white sky

colour never comes alone

I sleep on the banks of The River
the whole night it flows past me
silent and broad as blood

above lies the lichen of stars
night has tumbled her gravel

'People who have destroyed all their wildlife and live without it are not complete'

Chief Liabon (spiritual leader) of the Maasai (Kenya)

Milking the wild herd

Maasailand

By Dhyani Berger, with Paul Ntiati

Once upon a time, an old Maasai story goes, when women ruled over men, all wild herbivores belonged to women; as a result, the game that graze alongside Maasai livestock are still known as 'women's cattle' (see box). Today, Maasai women are regaining their power and, together with their children and menfolk, milking this wild herd. The purpose of our journey through Maasailand was to discover how this had come about, and to witness the impact of this reclaimed wealth on Maasai communities.

For me it was a return journey to places where I had tried to change the face of conservation in East Africa. What had become of the seeds I had helped to sow more than 25 years ago, when a small group of Maasai and development workers had begun to ask why the Maasai could not take an active part in conserving wildlife, and why they should not benefit from the animals they had lived with for generations? The Wildlife Extension Project (see box) had begun to help people regain access to resources lost when the national parks were created. Paul Ntiati, then the government range officer at the town of Loitokitok, became one of the key players in that initiative, and is still at the forefront of community conservation. Several of the people who would join us on our journey had

participated in those pioneering initiatives. They would all return to inspect the legacy of those early efforts; to see if yesterday's pastoralists had indeed become today's wildlife and forest managers.

We were to visit three areas, representing the ecology, land ownership and economic opportunity characteristic of Maasailand. The first was the Amboseli–Tsavo ecosystem at the foot of Mount Kilimanjaro, where Maasai group ranches lie within the wildlife dispersal area of the Amboseli and Tsavo West national parks. These parks are managed for the central government by the Kenya Wildlife Service (KWS). The second was the grasslands of the Maasai Mara, wildlife tourism capital of Kenya. Most Maasai in this area live on ranches bordering on the Mara Reserve, which is managed by the

How Maasai women lost their cattle

One day an eland was slaughtered. No woman would allow her children to go herding until they had tasted the sweetest meat, the liver. Since the Maasai had no tools for slaughtering, the exercise took so long that by the time they had eaten, all the wild animals had escaped into the bush. Women had lost their cattle as well as their power over men!

Narok County Council. The third was the sacred Naimina Enkiyo Forest on the Loita Highlands, home of the Laibon clan, keepers of Maasai spiritual tradition. This forest and nearby plains have remained communal land held in trust for the local Maasai community by the Narok County Council.

Nairobi, capital of Kenya, was once the heart of Maasailand, and visitors are greeted everywhere by images of the mythical Maasai warrior: on airport walls, at hotel reception desks, and in curio shops and kiosks on the crowded streets. But this ubiquitous image, exploited by the tourist industry, obscures the truth about the lives of these people and their links with the great East African parks: Amboseli, Maasai Mara and Serengeti. In reality they have been denied access to these parks for the past 50 years, and until recently have benefited minimally from wildlife-based tourism.

Fortunately the Maasai still occupy land adjacent to these parks, part of the vast grassland ecosystems that are still home to some of the greatest concentrations of wildlife on earth. The health of this ecosystem depends on the continued movement of wildlife between the parks and surrounding ranches; wildlife tourism has now extended from the protected areas on to nearby ranches, to the mutual benefit of parks and people.

Our first destination was Loitokitok, a bustling market town on the slopes of Kilimanjaro, where the Maasai mingle with neighbours and visitors selling everything from vegetables and shoes to religion. This was Ntiati's home, and the area where he and I had once worked together. We were joined by Nancy Kireu, another member of the original extension team and now associated with pastoralist women's education and community-based tourism.

From the town we could look down on to Amboseli Park and the Maasai ranches stretching to the distant Chyulu hills. We first headed for the park; we wanted to hear the story of Amboseli, a microcosm of Kenya's conservation history. Our storyteller would be Kurenta ole Nkutai, who was born in Amboseli and whose life reflects its history.

We met Nkutai and his second wife at their home at the Namelok irrigation scheme, not far from the park. Known as 'Professor' because of his wisdom, care in keeping records and an

The Wildlife Extension Project (WEP)

Extension work aimed at improving relations between the Maasai and the Kenyan wildlife authorities began in the mid-1970s, and gained momentum when the Wildlife Extension Project (WEP) was formed in 198x. Established by Dhyani Berger, author of this chapter, the WEP was aimed at strengthening the link between benefits and community initiative in conservation, in order to change government conservation policies and to demonstrate that parks could be managed not as islands but in conjunction with neighbouring land on to which wildlife moved seasonally. It was supported by Maasai and funded by NGOs.

From 1984 onwards the extension team, working closely with the Catholic Church, started a dialogue with Maasai on group ranches between Amboseli and Tsavo parks. Later this work spread to other parts of Maasailand and elsewhere in Kenya. The project helped to trigger major changes in conservation policy, including the formation of the Community Wildlife Service as part of the Kenya Wildlife Service (KWS), which was set up in 1990. Under this arrangement, community conservation wardens were posted to parks and wildlife areas. In 1997 the CWS became the partnership directorate in the KWS.

abiding interest in learning even though he never went to school, Nkutai was dressed in his best suit and carried a stick, as all Maasai elders do. We drove to the park across salty flats and past lush swamps, home to a variety of animal and bird life. On the way we saw wildebeest, zebra, a hyena walking purposefully by, and a huge elephant under an umbrella of acacias, silhouetted against a thunderous sky.

Nkutai took us to the place where he was born, now just a patch of grass, with a fallen log marking the site of the old homestead. Nearby, a clump of palm trees marked the entrance to the famous Amboseli Elephant Research Camp. We were in the heart of Amboseli.

'I was born here,' he recounted, 'at Oltukai Orok (the black palm), 49 years ago. The reserve was created when I was a small boy. I knew about it because Princess Margaret came to see the wildlife and the Maasai in the reserve. On that day cattle were allowed to drink water but not to graze nearby, as it would be too dusty for the princess.

'All the age groups went to welcome her. My father was invited because he was an elder. The chief at that time was Kipelian ole Kirisia of the *Iltareto* age group [that of Jomo Kenyatta, Kenya's first president].

When the elders were sitting with the princess, they asked each other, 'Why has she come?' They did not know. There were a few tourist camps here at that time. One white man had asked the elders to give him a campsite, and Chief Kirisia received a gift of a bull for doing so. The princess went to see those camps, which were in the central part of the reserve.

'My father said at that time that these people might be coming to protect this land and conserve this place for the Maasai. I have been waiting all my life in the hope that that thing will happen as my father told me...'

To the Maasai, at that time, the threat of losing their land was inconceivable:

'We did not believe the land could ever be taken way — because it was our land, and isn't even good land for keeping livestock. We used it

only as a refuge during the dry season, when there were lots of pods from trees and plenty of grass. The wildlife did not threaten our pastoralist way of life. It was possible to protect both wildlife and cattle in the same place.

'When this land was turned into a game reserve it didn't interfere with our livelihood, and therefore we didn't regard this as a threat. The threats came when a new leader, Oloitipitip, supported the declaration of the swamps which were part of the reserve as a park.'

Later, Nkutai continued his story while seated on a tree stump on Observation Hill, overlooking a panorama of shimmering swamps and mirages with Mount Kilimanjaro as a backdrop.

'Our age set, *Ilkishumu*, were *morans* (warriors) from 1967 until 1976 when we graduated as elders. I was assistant to the *Olanguanani* (age set leader), Ole Musa. We were still *moran* when the park was formed. A meeting was held with the minister for wildlife and tourism, the director of wildlife (the latter a Maasai), and Oloitipitip (then a Maasai

member of parliament). My father was chosen to speak, as was Ole Musa. We were told to leave the park, and to wait for the rains and move out. We were told we would be provided with water outside the park, but after the rains people refused to go as they also had to have access to salt licks.

'So that is how it happened... After the park was created, Oloitipitip was promoted to full cabinet minister.'

What difference did this make to the Maasai?

'Attitudes to wildlife changed ... In the past, when people were killed or injured by wildlife they thought that was just an accident. No one was responsible because it was a part of life here. But when the land became the property of government, it changed because the owners of wildlife should be responsible – and provide compensation, if people are attacked or killed. You cannot own wildlife and say you are not responsible for its actions.'

The Maasai accepted the park under certain conditions, but did the government keep to those conditions?

'They never have until now. They tried to pipe water from Serena spring on to the plains outside the park, but both the design and the way they did it could not work. The community was not consulted.'

So what has been the outcome? The Maasai feel the government has failed to keep its word to provide water and financial benefits. The water outside the park is not always enough, and they continue periodically to bring their cattle into the park for water, salt and grazing. Relations between the park and its neighbours have fluctuated over the years, depending on the weather and the personality and style of park managers. NGOs began working to promote dialogue, culminating in 1984 in the establishment of the WEP (see box). The Olgulului Group Ranch chose Nkutai to work as conservation action leader with the WEP. Until 1989 he played a key role in the organisation, working to protect wildlife and the environment.

He explained: 'Maasai interest in conservation is really about the use of resources, so I stressed the need to protect not only wildlife but also trees, springs, water catchment areas, river banks, dry river beds, and even hills from overexploitation.'

His work with the WEP demonstrated the potential for partnership between communities and conservationists. By the end of the decade, the Maasai around Amboseli were not only actively protecting their environment, but also earning from wildlife by negotiating more equitable contracts with tour operators who had built camps on their land.

The work of Nkutai and his colleagues laid the foundation for the community wildlife service which formed part of the KWS when it was established in 1990. Kenneth Nashuu, another member of WEP, who would join us in Mara, became the community wildlife warden at Amboseli, and Nkutai took charge of game scouts on group ranches. The KWS paid scouts from park revenue which was now shared with group ranches. Kurenta stressed the contribution to be made by community-based scouts:

'Our game scouts are responsible for monitoring wildlife in the Amboseli wildlife dispersal zone; they link community conservation efforts and protected area management. They should be consulted and represented in forums such as the KWS, the district development committee and on group ranch committees, to influence decisions on how resources should be managed.'

When asked to talk about the challenges facing community conservation and ecotourism, Nkutai raised the question of leadership, a theme which recurred regularly throughout our journey.

'Leadership is now a challenge for conservation. The institutions in charge have changed. And if somebody cuts down a tree, it has to be reported to a government chief, who may have no concern for conservation. The group ranch committee, not the government,

should be given that responsibility. There were indigenous systems to manage those resources, which could guide these committees.'

We had heard that a change in leadership within the kws had also undermined efforts made by community scouts. Funds for community programmes and salaries of scouts had been withheld, illustrating the vulnerability of conservation overly dependent on government support. We were told that group ranches were not prepared to pay the community scouts, despite their earnings from tourism. Commented Nkutai:

'How can you give people responsibility for resources, and yet they are not employed? People were not paid in the past, but it is different now because group ranches were formed to commercialise the use of resources; therefore, economic factors should now be considered.'

He called for national policy and programmes to acknowledge and support community conservation and to integrate the contribution of the Maasai, who were, after all, the custodians of wildlife long before the modern conservation era. Mr. Kiio, the kws warden at Amboseli, echoed this view, saying that, in his view, the survival of Amboseli depended on partnership.

'We have to manage the entire system ... We need to integrate land use planning for park and surrounding land involving all those responsible for overseeing and using natural resources – particularly the swamps, springs and rivers flowing off Kilimanjaro. Kurenta and his colleagues are essential to this process.'

We left the park to find out how the original inhabitants of the area, the Maasai, were benefiting from the Amboseli tourism bonanza. Driving on to the Olgulului Group Ranch nearby, there was no gate and no visible boundary. We approached a village. It looked like any other, a circle of mud and dung huts surrounding an open space where livestock were housed at night. However, this village had been built as a 'cultural *boma*' [village] to earn income from tourists.

We then saw something unusual: two crescents of red-clad people stood between trees beyond the village. A small group walked slowly along the line, and as they passed each person he or she would sit down. A feeling of suspense was in the air. 'They are counting votes,' we were told; in fact, we were witnessing the election of the *boma* chairman. The counters reached the end of the second crescent. There was a brief discussion, followed by an announcement, and then an explosion of colour as the winner was lifted up high while jubilant supporters sang and ran in great leaps, with spears and sticks held high. We were witnessing a blend of old and new; an election with a distinctly Maasai flavour.

The vote had been close: 166 to 146. The participation of 312 people seemed evidence of a true community-based enterprise. We were to learn more about the organisation and value of cultural *bomas* from Daniel Leturresh, chairman of a neighbouring cultural *boma*, with whom we were to spend the night.

With the election over, the Enkongu-Ookankere *boma* was back in business. Several minibuses arrived, and tourists were ushered into the village, where they were invited into huts to see how the Maasai lived. Women had laid out their crafts for sale. We admired the beaded necklaces as tourists bargained over prices.

Warriors began to perform a rhythmic song, leaping and landing with flat-footed thumps – much to the delight of the onlookers, who were taking photographs and joining in amid encouraging laughter. Before our departure we paid our entrance fee of 1 000 Kenyan shillings a person to a serious young man.

That evening we camped under huge acacia trees next to Leturresh's village at Esiteti Hill, a famous viewsite overlooking the salt pans of 'Lake' Amboseli. This is an exclusive concession area rented by the group ranch to a safari company. Leturresh and other elders welcomed us, and we sat around a fire deep into the night. We heard singing in the village, and joined the dancer after

clambering over huge branches laid across its entrance as a barrier to lion and other intruders.

The next morning we awoke to the sound of bells, as cattle left the village. Leturresh, chair of the Enkongu Narok cultural *boma* for the past 10 years, spoke about cultural businesses at Amboseli.

'We started the cultural *bomas* to tap the benefits of wildlife. In the past, income from tourism was not going to the grass roots – it went to government and, to some extent, the group ranch leaders. Since we started these cultural villages, even the poorer people have access to money. The benefits go directly to members.

'In the past, tourists were keen to visit our villages; almost every village became a tourist destination. So we thought it would be better to find a central place where we could control the business, so that our culture would not be degraded.'

We wanted to know how these businesses had affected local communities; he particularly highlighted the impact on women.

'It has helped women to become a little more independent. They used to rely on their husbands to provide sugar and other essentials. Now, it has kind of put a voice in women. They can buy what they want, using the money they earn from their crafts, which is not controlled by the men.'

Also, wildlife was now seen as a community resource: 'People now know the value of wildlife. Tourists come not only for the culture, but for wildlife as well. If we have plenty of wildlife, then we will have visitors ... so it contributes to the wellbeing of the people. This is a concession area which we lease to tour operators. We have agreed that they will use the land for occasional tented camps, but that we will continue to live here as pastoralists.'

There are five cultural villages near Amboseli; according to Leturresh, they each earn about 400 000 Kenyan shillings a year. However, some of this revenue is lost to tour drivers who charge tourists a fee for visiting villages. To overcome this exploitative practice, Leturresh spoke

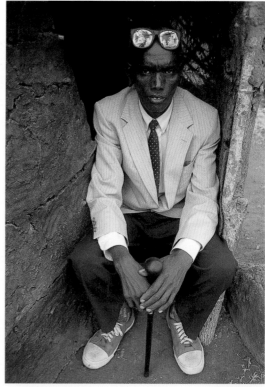

of a need for cultural village associations to negotiate payment directly with tour companies.

We wanted to know how income earned by the *bomas* was shared.

'The *boma* committee decides how to spend the money, but it has to communicate with the community. The committee has to report earnings at the annual general meeting, and explain how moneys are spent. The herders who care for our cattle are paid, we pay bursaries for children in school, and if there is any other need we address it. If necessary, we provide food relief. We agree at the end of each year what each member should get.'

We asked whether members knew how much money their group ranch, Olgulului, was earning from other sources of income: the concession area, the community campsite, the lodge, and kws revenue-sharing.

'We don't know,' Leturresh said, 'as we are not told by the group ranch committee what has been paid and how much has been used. The Amboseli–Tsavo Association [of group ranches] suffers from the same problem of accountability. Elected representatives should consult constantly with the members, because it is here where local issues and needs of the members are supposed to be addressed – but this is not happening.'

Having witnessed the election at the neighbouring *boma*, we wanted to hear Leturresh's views on leadership. He explained that choosing leaders traditionally was a lengthy consultative process. However, cultural villages were registered as formal organisations, so choosing leaders was neither traditional nor modern – it was something in between. 'What you saw yesterday was really a mixture of old and new ways.' Government officials had been present to monitor the election. A meeting had first been held where the rules laid down by the department of social services had been explained.

The entry of the Maasai community into the monetary economy has had a significant impact on quality of leadership, as the shift from selection to election has weakened its leadership.

'Nowadays, leaders are sometimes corrupt,' Leturresh said frankly. 'People are using money, especially group ranch money, to buy support. Also, the government (and the modern institutions it promotes) are choosing chiefs in a different way and that is why we are experiencing problems.'

A reminder of the need to bridge the gap between leaders and community was a story told by Thomas Kasaine, secretary of Eselenkei Group Ranch, on our way back to Nairobi. The leaders of this ranch had set aside land as a wildlife conservation area and had made a deal with a tour operator.

However, this had been a mistake: 'We thought the community understood and were behind us,' said Thomas, 'but we were wrong. We have had to ask the operator to close down his camp, and are going back to the members.' (The problem was eventually resolved; the Eselenkei Conservation Area reopened six months later.)

Another problem surrounding community leadership structures is the absence of women. We were alerted to this by Lucy Nashuu, who welcomed us at a settlement at Inkisanjani on Kuku Group Ranch. She was in charge of the homestead as her husband, Kenneth, was away working as a partnership officer for the kws (he would join us later on our journey). Once a nursery school teacher, Lucy was now managing the family herd, an irrigated garden, and planning to open a *posho* (maize) mill. She had once led a woman's group that captured the tourist trade on the much-travelled route between Amboseli and Tsavo parks.

'There are no women on the group ranch committee,' she declared. 'As women we are sidelined, because our leaders don't recognise women, unless somebody like me goes to them. They are trying now to accept us. We would like to take part in deciding how money earned by the ranch is used.'

Nashuu talked about how settlement and agriculture had affected the environment around her home.

'There are a lot of changes, and much to be done to protect the environment. People have not understood that we need all natural things. A lot of people are coming to dig *shambas* [gardens], and the Maasai and also others are felling trees at a great rate. The chiefs are failing to tell the people how this affects the environment.

'We cannot stop people, because they can claim certain areas as their own. You know, on a group ranch everybody has a portion and he fences it and cuts trees to make *shambas*. Also, outsiders can fell trees without the knowledge of the owners. A few who understand are seeing that it will be a mess in future.

'We used to get firewood just here, but now we have to walk for about two hours. You see, as women we are below the husband. Even if we tell them not to cut wood, they say, "Aha – a woman cannot come and tell me."

'Right now you find greedy people putting their livestock in the dry season grazing area; within two months everything is over. The chiefs and rich people have many cattle feeding in conservation areas. Some people make very big *olopololis* [dry season/calf grazing areas] of 100 acres, and nobody cares to tell them to make it smaller so there's room for others. You find it fenced; you cannot enter someone else's *olopololi*. Overgrazing is everywhere. The elders are doing nothing … communities need to be sensitised.'

The potential for responsible community management of resources was clear from her description of efforts to manage irrigation.

'Water is not a problem, because we have springs. We are doing a lot to conserve them, even going as far as fencing them with the help of SARDEP (the Semi Arid Rural Development Programme). We are also planning to cement our irrigation furrows; right now we are contributing to buy cement.

'We have to share water … Every furrow has a committee which also includes women. We don't want committees without women.'

She also gave us her views on wildlife:

'We, the community, are the best owners of wildlife because we live with it. Overall the KWS is in charge of protecting wildlife and people's lives, as people are as important as wildlife.

'Wildlife has benefited us in numerous ways. Revenue from the parks is shared with group ranches, and has been used to pay school fees of poor children and to drill boreholes. They have promised to give us more, but they say what they get is not enough.'

We spoke of the practicalities of coexisting with wild animals. 'We coexist nicely,' she said, but then admitted that zebras invaded the maize fields at night. She felt the KWS should fence the area to keep out dangerous animals, as it has done elsewhere.

Later we heard a warrior had been killed by an elephant. We had arrived at the village of Paul Kinyala, former chairman of the Kuku Group Ranch. He looked tired as he came to greet us, having just returned home after two days in the bush tracking the elephant with KWS and community scouts. 'It was a bull elephant known to us,' he explained; 'it had given us problems before. It took 24 hours to find it and shoot it.'

Kinyala gave us information about revenue from wildlife earned by the ranch. Each year Kuku received between 150 000 and 400 000 Kenyan shillings from the KWS. The ranch also earned revenue from a camp at Oldonyo Sambu, leased by a Canadian as a training centre. The people from this campsite helped children to go to school. About 20 Maasai were employed at this camp and another at Iltilal.

In our quest to trace the legacy of early extension work, we spent a night in the Chyulu Hills not far from Ntiati's home on Imbirikani Group Ranch. Here, in the mid-1980s, the WEP team had facilitated the first well-negotiated lease between a group ranch and a tour operator.

A young Kenyan, Richard Bonham, had found an ideal site for a safari camp and wanted to rent the land. The WEP had helped the Maasai and Bonham to communicate and then negotiate a contract. Bonham built a small exclusive lodge in the hills with hopes for a long-term relationship with the ranch. Nearly 13 years later, the partnership is still intact.

Besides paying an annual concession fee, Bonham has helped the ranch establish a conservation trust to promote sustainable ranch management. Trust projects have included dams and boreholes, afforestation, school development, school bursaries, and wildlife cropping.

At the centre of the ranch is a village zone with a primary school and line of *dukas* (shops), surrounded by homesteads scattered on the dry plains. The office of the Community Conservation Trust is hidden in a grove of trees. A meeting was in progress between Bonham and the new group ranch committee. Afterwards, Noah Ntiati, Paul's brother, took me around the compound. He was bursting with pride. We remembered the first tiny tree nursery he had started in 1984. Now he pointed out homes in the distance, all shaded with trees. When the community had first settled here, to be close to water from a pipeline, it had soon run out of fuel and building materials. Now tree planting has become a normal part of life for these cattle keepers.

We were invited to spend the evening with Bonham and his family. We drove out of the village zone, passing cattle, tail-flicking tommy (gazelle) and giraffe, crossed the grassy plains, and climbed up to the soft rounded shapes of the Chyulu Hills. Sundowners with Jackson ole Sakimpa, Bonham's right-hand man, on a wide verandah at Oldonyo Wuas Lodge provided a breathtaking view of Kili, towering above the hazy rangelands. Over dinner we heard stories of ups and downs over the years – but the lodge is still there, providing solid proof that partnerships can work.

Land use and ownership

By the time Kenya became independent in 1963, Maasailand, like all communal areas, had been placed under the trusteeship of local authorities, primarily Kajiado and Narok county councils. These councils held the land 'in trust' for communities, but were given powers to set aside land for public purposes, including conservation. Amboseli had been a national reserve from 1948 until 1961 when it was handed over to the Kajiado County Council to become the Amboseli Maasai Game Reserve, administered by the council. Similarly, administration of the Maasai Mara Game Reserve was handed over to the Narok County Council. Early on, indigenous communities in reserves were permitted to continue seasonal livestock grazing; however, no human activity was permitted in parks. When gazetted in 1976, Amboseli Park was formed from a small part of the reserve around the swamps (vital to the Maasai in the dry season), and its administration was taken over by the central government. Remaining reserve land was adjudicated (privatised) into group ranches, owned jointly by Maasai communities with single title deeds, and managed by elected management committees. There are six group ranches in the larger ecosystem of southern Kajiado District surrounding Amboseli Park and stretching as far as Tsavo West and the Chyulu parks in the east. It was here that the WEP carried out the core of its work in 1984-1989.

The Maasai Mara remains a reserve under the Narok County Council. Despite this, livestock was banned from the reserve in the 1980s when the council began to earn major revenue from tourism. Some of the communal land adjacent to Mara has been privatised into individual or group ranches.

On the way back to Nairobi we passed through central Kajiado, where the Maasai have divided group ranches into small individual holdings, sold much land to outsiders, and have so lost most of their wildlife.

We climbed up into the highlands until we looked down on the Great Rift Valley, a vast, hazy gash in the earth several hundred kilometres long, stretching north to Lake Baringo and south into Tanzania via Lake Natron. We then crossed the valley towards the Mau escarpment and climbed up into Narok District, known not only for the Maasai Mara but also for its wheat tycoons, many of whom are Maasai. The bustling town of Narok is the gateway to the highland plateau, which supports a huge mechanised agricultural industry. In this region agriculture competes directly with tourism as a form of land use; here, the Maasai way of life has been hugely influenced by the cash economy.

Kenneth Nashuu joined us for the rest of our journey; Ntiati was to leave us after Maasai Mara. A founding member of the wep, Nashuu has

come a long way since 1985; from group ranch conservation activist to kws partnership officer responsible for community conservation throughout Narok District.

Leaving Narok town, we were soon travelling towards distant blue hills across plains covered with whistling thorn bush. Maasai villages, herds of livestock and wildlife cohabited peacefully along the way, giving an inkling of what was to come.

The Maasai Mara lies at the northern tip of the greater Serengeti ecosystem, which extends south into Tanzania. Like Amboseli, Mara has no fenced boundary between itself and neighbouring Maasai ranches, or between Kenya and Tanzania; herds of game move freely back and forth. As the Maasai burn their land annually to kill ticks and encourage the growth of new grass, concentrations of wildlife tend to move to neighbouring ranches at certain times of the year.

We wanted to hear about the relationship between local communities and the reserve, and meet Maasai who earn revenue from tourism on these ranches. Collaboration between Maasai

leaders and safari companies goes back to the days of the big game hunters more than 50 years ago. These old associations led to the establishment of famous camps, such as Governors. Over the past 15 years, tourist companies have been searching for more pristine camping spots on private land, away from the 'madding crowd' inside the reserve; now, more than 20 companies lease land on Koiyaki and other neighbouring ranches. These companies recently formed the Campfire Association (not to be confused with Zimbabwe's Campfire programme), aimed at strengthening their partnership with the Maasai in conserving and managing wildlife and marketing tourism.

We entered the Mara at Sekanani Gate to pay our respects to the warden, a Maasai like the majority of Narok County Council employees in the reserve. For many years, little of the money earned by the reserve had gone to the local Maasai. In 1991, a KWS revenue-sharing policy stipulated that 25 per cent of protected area earnings should go directly to local people. The council had been reluctant to pay all ranches, and one group successfully fought a court case to earn its share from the Mara.

We drove through the reserve to Riverside Campsite at Talek, midway along the eastern border with Koiyaki Group Ranch. I had worked here with Friends of Conservation in the early 1990s, taking the first difficult steps in helping ordinary people organise themselves to benefit from the reserve. Ntiati had been based here in 1998, helping to build a co-operative relationship between the Maasai and tour operators. More recently, working with the African Conservation Centre, he has been helping Maasai to form a camp owners' association.

Talek trading centre is a node for entrepreneurship; it serves tour bus drivers and hotel employees as much as the Maasai people who have settled close to the reserve's boundary. In 1970 there was only one Maasai village here; now, there are three lodges and at least 11 Maasai-owned campsites in the vicinity. Local leaders such as Chief ole Saiyalel have taken advantage of tourism opportunities. In the early 1990s this enterprising man piped in water, installed a water tank, and built latrines, cooking areas and a shop. Now he has expanded his operation to include bungalows, a bar, and a dining area. There is ample space for overland trucks; the evening when we arrived a group of 25 travellers were being attended to by friendly and capable staff fluent in English and able to communicate in several other tourist languages.

Sitting together over a bottle of soda, the chief told us his story. Pointing to his extended lobes looped over the upper ear, he proudly said:

'Look... I am a typical Maasai. I never went to school. I grew up looking after cattle grazing alongside wildlife. When outsiders first came here to see wildlife, we didn't know their value, but we now know we are sitting next to a pot of gold.

'I started as a night watchman at Fig Tree Camp inside the Mara in the year *Mzee* Kenyatta died [1978]. I saw what the owner did, and asked myself: why can't I do the same? He started with four tents; today I already have more. Everyone has their time, and now my time has come.'

We were told that 11 members of Koiyaki Group Ranch had established campsites on this ranch near Talek. The next day we accompanied ole Njaanga, the local county councillor, to one of these sites. Intrigued by these initiatives, we wanted to know more about community-based tourism efforts.

We learned that Maasai land owners bordering the reserve had set aside Koiyaki and half of Lemek group ranches for tourism, and registered the Koiyaki-Lemek Conservation Trust. Members have agreed not to fence their land, and to protect wildlife. Besides benefiting from game viewing fees charged by the trust, about 25 village clusters are now benefiting directly from contracts with tour operators who lease sites nearby. The trust has an office, vehicles, a manager, and game scouts who take care of wildlife.

We visited David Mposia, a game scout on Koiyaki. He told us that Maasai youths take up this work with enthusiasm, as they understand and do not fear animals. In the past young men would prove their prowess by killing a lion, but today they recognise a lion has more value alive than dead. Recently, he said, warriors had come across a lion with its paw caught in a snare. Instead of killing it, they covered the lion's head with a blanket, and cut the snare to release it.

We met leaders of the recently registered Koiyaki Camp Owners Association (KOCOA) under a thatched roof shelter at Riverside Camp. They said they had, under Ntiati's guidance, formed an association so that they would become known as a group, inside or outside the country. 'Our aim is to avoid being exploited. We are now collecting booking fees and bed night levies directly from the Campfire Association, instead of someone else acting for us.'

Income from tourism is clearly a reality for some of the Maasai of Mara. A local development worker told us that the money was being spent on leisure, schools, buying livestock, and marrying more wives. 'They may build a small house, buy a second-hand vehicle or start a campsite. Some Maasai have become tycoons, with several cars and more than a thousand head of livestock. Most of these guys have not gone to school, but they are damn rich and send their children to expensive private schools and universities. They are investing in education because they lacked it themselves.'

We had spoken to the men – leaders and others active in conservation. But what were the experiences and views of ordinary folk, particularly women?

Not far from Talek is Enkiyio Enkorien Cultural Village, built by the Mpuai Women's Group. A gracious old lady, Leksua Kool, explained how they had started their business:

'We built the village in three months. Each wife constructed her own house, but the Maasai are not jealous people, so they help each other.

The members come from different families; some of them from far places. Members come here regularly, but not without the leave of the men, because they have to collect firewood and fetch water.

'We sell ornaments to tourists. We use our language, and welcome them with a dance. They become very interested.

'We like this village because we get money to do what we want. In someone's village women are under men, but here they are free because if they get 2 000 shillings they can use it how they want. Also, they can help a man to buy medicine for cows and can take care of the family in case there is not enough money … We are no longer disturbing men for money. For instance, children are under their moms. If a child is chased from school and asked to bring 200 shillings, the mom can provide that 200.

'We also get money from entrance fees. Every tourist who visits the village pays 600 shillings. We save this money until there is enough, and buy cattle which we sell later.

'We have our own account. The councillor has donated 30 000 shillings, and we are saving money in case of problems. We are also thinking about getting a plot at Talek and building a shop there.'

Members of the group spoke of how life was changing. One woman said her first-born had not

The wildebeest migration

Every year, more than a million animals trek for 500 kilometres through the Serengeti–Mara ecosystem. They start off from the short grass plains in Tanzania, through woodlands, mating on the way. They reach the Mara at the peak of the dry season, where there is still enough green grass to fatten the females, now heavy with calf. At the beginning of the short rains in November, this huge population moves back across the border to calve on the Serengeti plains.

gone to school, but now they had the money to send another son to school.

We were welcomed into the village with a song, and invited for a cup of sweet milky tea. We bought multicoloured necklaces and a beaded stick, and received bracelets in turn. Already aware of the value of marketing, members asked us to send them clients from Namibia.

Having spoken to those who had long struggled to regain rights over wildlife and were now beginning to benefit from that resource, we wanted to experience what Maasai Mara is most famous for: its wildlife. Mara did not let us down. Within two days we had seen it all; golden plains teeming with wildlife, sunset silhouettes, and one of the greatest spectacles on earth: the wildebeest migration.

At a picnic lunch under a balanities tree we watched streams of wildebeest racing by. Following them to a lookout above the Mara River, we watched a cascade of glistening bodies pour down the banks and mill around in

confusion on the beach until one individual leapt into the water, followed by a gyrating stream of animals which swam across the river and scrambled past us up the bank. There was a din of grunts and bleats, with mothers and calves trying to reunite, running back and forth along the line, often against the tide.

Driving out of the reserve, we passed cattle walking back to their villages for the night – a reminder that pastoralists have long played their part in creating this prolific paradise. Indeed, the burning of grass and the movement of cattle herds still contribute to keeping the grasslands open. In the past the Maasai were nomads, adopting a resource use strategy that mimicked wildlife migrations. Nowadays, however, they are settled with their livestock along the reserve boundary and can no longer easily follow their wildlife 'cousins'. Still, wildlife, people and domestic animals continue to live in relative harmony. The Maasai are indeed milking the wild

herd – but, given the increasingly central role played by tourism, can the environment sustain the intensive use? What will be the future of the big herds: wildlife, cattle – and tourists?

The last leg of our journey took us on to the Loita Highlands, where the Naimina Enkiyio Forest covers the Nguruman escarpment which drops steeply down to Lake Magadi in the Rift Valley. Here the spiritual heritage of the Maasai is proudly preserved, under the tutelage of the *laibons* (seers and ritual experts) of the Kidongi clan who have long been consulted for their wisdom. The forest is a cultural sanctuary where ceremonies central to the continuation of Maasai tradition and the ordering of their society are practised.

Our arrival at Loita coincided with *Eturruj*, a rare ceremony that marks the passage of elderhood, and shifts authority at each level of the age set system. We were to witness the retirement of the senior elder age group, *Ilnyangusi*, and the assumption of responsibility by the *Iseuri* group who would become senior elders in turn.

We arrived at Ole Kalu's village, entering the cattle stockade in time for a feast. Men gathered around a 'table' of olive leaves heaped with roasted meat were distributing hunks of meat to *Ilnyangusi* seated along the inner fence, who were chewing with relish. I was intrigued by the dexterity with which the old guys sliced pieces of meat off the bone with their razor-sharp knives. The carvers, who must have been *Iseuri*, invited me to squat in their circle, handing me prize pieces which I enjoyed. '*Ashe oleng*!' I felt welcome, although I was the only woman among them.

Some time later, women in fine beadwork began to dance past the seated *wazee* (old men), stopping every now and then to face them and sing their praises. The leader, perhaps the first wife of the host, carried a pot of red ochre mixed with fat. She and a second wife smeared the brow of each old man. The song was compelling and I was drawn in to join the line, raising a smile of appreciation from the old fellows.

The ceremony drew to an end. The *Iseuri*, who would henceforth bear the responsibilities of

eldership, whose knowledge of ancient lore would be drawn upon and who would have to face the challenges of guiding their people into the modern age, began to sing and pass along the line of retirees, who rose to their feet and joined the end of the moving line. Slowly the men, now joined by the women, wound out of the stockade and village on to the surrounding plain. The two age groups then turned to face one another, and for the last time shared their dance. Gradually the retired elders moved away to sit under a distant thorn tree.

The ceremony over, we greeted old friends and consumed mugs of sweetened tea, gratefully received after standing in the cold wind. We then visited the village of Charles Saitabu, a former colleague, before we returned to Ilkerin, Loita's development centre, for the night. This was where I had worked with Saibatu in the mid-1990s to collect local plants and document indigenous plant knowledge and use. Ethnobotany had been a first step towards grounding modern management of the Naimina Enkiyio Forest in local hands, as the forest is vital to local livelihood. Many people who are settled along the fringe and others based far out on the rangelands use it as a dry season refuge. Also, people, their livestock and wild animals depend on springs and rivers deep in the forest, as there are no permanent rivers on the rangelands north west of the forest.

For several years the Iloitai Maasai have been in a tug of war with the Narok County Council, which wants to have the forest declared as a reserve and develop it for tourism. However, any indication of plans to open the forest to mass tourism and channel benefits mainly to outsiders is perceived locally as a threat. Unlike most of the land at Mara and Loitokitok, which is privately owned by groups, Loita has remained communal land under control of the local authority – hence its vulnerability to being annexed by the council.

To forestall the council's plans, the Loitan leaders had registered the Naimina Enkiyio Conservation Trust in order to vest control of the forest in the hands of the people who live around and use it. We hoped to trace progress made in securing local ownership of the forest, and in planning for community-based forest and tourism management. We first wanted to speak to Mkompo Ole Simel, chief *laibon*, ritual expert, soothsayer, caretaker of the forest, member of the council of elders, and also chairman of the trust.

Joyce Nasieku, a local filmmaker and former member of the ethnobotany team, took us to look for Mkompo. We found him at his village in Kisakon, a valley running deep into Naimina Enkiyio. A few years ago he had blessed our ethnobotany work. He invited us to talk to him at his home nestled among trees on the forest fringe.

Wearing a monkeyskin cloak with a royal purple lining, he spoke of his work as a *laibon* and the significance of the forest and wildlife for the health and happiness of the Maasai community.

'First, the forest is important culturally as that is where special ceremonies are held. All age sets are led through and blessed in the forest. Second, the rain comes from the trees. It provides us with water. We are controlling the cutting of trees in the forest so that future generations will also be able to use it. Wildlife in the forest is an asset. Tourists come to see it, and our people benefit from it.'

We asked him who should manage forest resources, and whether youths with modern education had a part to play.

'The Maasai should manage their own resources,' he replied. 'They should be the ones in the forefront. We need forest managers who are educated but also spiritually oriented, and who understand the value of our forest to our culture.'

Did women have something special to offer in caring for the forest? He laughed and asked Joyce Nasieku to speak, agreeing with her answer.

'Women play a central role,' she said, 'because they are the people who normally go to the forest to collect water, grass, firewood and herbs for children. Women use trees, but don't cut them down. They should be the first to be given responsibility for managing the forest.'

Mkompo recognised the mixed blessings brought by tourism: the income from tourism was beneficial, but he also feared the impact of the monetary economy on young people and the Maasai way of life. The possible loss of the forest made him suspicious of newly arriving tour companies. 'Thus we need a tight partnership among Loita leaders to identify anyone with bad intentions, and to ensure that the forest is protected and the community benefits.'

An international NGO was helping local leaders to draw up their own forest management plan and also to establish a form of ownership of their land. 'As a Maasai, you have to brand a cow to know that it is yours. We want to brand this land by registering it as group ranches so that we can say, this is our land.'

At the end of the interview, Mkompo's elder wife brought him a gourd and a skin to sit on. He talked softly, shaking the gourd, emptying out little stones of many colours on to the skin, counting them and sorting them into groups before refilling the gourd and throwing them again. 'I am happy you came. I was looking to see whether you brought any bad omen or any bad intentions, but you are clean. You are welcome to return…' Mkompo's wife brought us sweet milky tea to send us on our way.

Not far from the *laibon*'s house is the home of James and Esther Kone. We drove across country, through a dry swamp, to their homestead tucked into the side of a hill, overlooking the great green sweep of Kisokon valley with its scattered houses, maize fields and cattle herds.

As we approached we heard the sound of the wind chimes I had left with James when I set out for Namibia. He had come to my house with the *laibon* and other elders to bless my journey.

James declared that the winds of Loita would blow through these chimes until I returned. No wonder I was back, to find him at home reading an article about conservancies in Namibia.

We were welcomed with open arms and invited to drink *kule naoto* (sour milk) from a huge beaded gourd. We talked of Loita affairs, and the deep concern James and others felt for the future of this forest and its people. The possibility of outside interests controlling the use of the forest was still a real fear.

Central to the debate about the ownership of Naimina Enkiyio is the growth and control of tourism. For many years, before the explosion in commercial tourism, Loita attracted a small number of visitors. Now, companies specialising in adventure tourism bring small groups to walk and ride on horseback through the forest. Some Loitans have become accomplished guides and are making a good living from this work. But plans to generate more economic benefits from the forest must strike a balance between rewarding individual entrepreneurship and local communities. This is an issue affecting Moses Kipelian, another member of the ethnobotany team and a master guide who has taken people into the forest for more than 20 years.

We arrived at Kipelian's *boma* as he was preparing for a trip with a group of Dutch hikers. Porters and guides decked out in Maasai regalia were preparing huge loads, strapping on backpacks and organising tough-looking Europeans clad in hiking boots, cameras and sun hats. Amid the hustle and bustle we were welcomed with a cup of *chai* for an intense conversation, graciously interrupted by a flow of requests and instructions as the leader organised his men.

These forest guides expressed concern about progress in forest and tourism management planning. In their view, neither the local development agency nor the international NGO had adequately consulted and involved forest users, and neither had they built on community

ethnobotany work. They felt sidelined, perceiving the NGO's efforts to be externally focused and aligned with groups in Loita who did not have the best interests of the community at heart. This was a different view from that expressed by the *laibon*, and their perceptions raised questions about communication between the leaders, both customary and developmental, and the general populace in Loita.

Later discussions with the NGO team revealed good intentions gone awry, and perhaps a failure to communicate enough and develop a common understanding with different interest groups. The NGO had been given funds for preliminary information-gathering and consultation, as a preliminary step to designing a forest management planning project. Aware of the conflict with the council, and internal differences in Loita, spokespersons told us that they had to remain 'neutral' – and so avoided associating with people who had been key players in the past!

In Loita we were reminded that communities are not homogeneous entities but are fragmented into subgroups with different views, marked by complex internal associations and conflicts. We witnessed the challenges faced by an outside agency with resources for a short-term intervention and with a limited background on local social dynamics.

We left Loita pondering fundamental questions that have to be addressed by all those promoting and managing community-based tourism. How should local rights to control and benefit from tourism be balanced with external and different internal interests? Our last interview with Kenneth Nashuu gave us an insight into the strong forces that influence these decisions in the Maasai community. He spoke of the power of the elite.

'The majority, who are poor, have little say in the Maasai community. If the rich people see that it will benefit them to keep the forest intact, they can still do it. The leaders control everything.

The elite are those owning a large number of animals, such as cattle and goats, and a large number of anything else, including big houses.

'As a man in the Maasai community, you have to build your capacity in terms of what you own; you cannot address the community without it. You have to own something for the Maasai to recognise you.'

This confirmed the point made by many people on the journey, that one of the greatest challenges facing the Maasai is finding capable and just leadership. In the Maasai tradition, leaders are not only respected for their wisdom but also for their wealth. This seems to give some leaders a licence to use public money for their own advancement. By contrast, community-based management and the use of resources in the modern setting call for a democratic social system, and a more equitable distribution of wealth.

Nashuu explained that one task of extension workers such as himself was to address leadership and equity issues via training aimed at raising awareness among different socio-economic groups about their rights and responsibilities.

'One answer is to design a system in which equity or the sharing of resources will be built in, so that less fortunate people will benefit. But it is not an easy job to pass through the elite and say, This property or this sum of money should go to the poor. The thing is to make people aware and combine those two forces: the elite and the poor. We use our training system, involving exercises and games, to get people to think about their own behaviour, and how much they take at the expense of others.'

Kurenta, Leturresh, Mkompo and many others spoke about the values of respect and wisdom instilled via the age set structure. In the past, youths learned to be responsible members of society through training and ceremonies that marked passages and shifted responsibility in an ordered manner from one age group to another. They observed that the impersonal transfer of

authority from tribal people to the government had led to moral values being eroded, and leaders becoming increasingly irresponsible. Many people told us that modern development models disregarded the indigenous systems that had sustained community and the natural resources on which they depended in the past.

Nashuu also pointed out that the future of the Maasai as wildlife managers and active participants in the tourism industry depended not only on social dynamics but also on national policy. A flaw in present policy was a restriction to non-consumptive use in the form of tourism. Given the political turmoil in Kenya, tourism had plummeted and communities dependent on wildlife-based tourism were suffering. Communities thus needed to diversify sources of income away from wildlife.

He stressed the urgency of a proper policy framework and legislation. Despite the progressive community conservation programme initiated in 1990, when the CWS was established, there was still no legislation that supported the devolution of wildlife use rights and accompanying management responsibilities. In his view, inconsistent policies and programme support for community conservation over the last 10 years reflected a lack of government commitment to giving communities a significant management role.

Besides this, it appears as if the ambivalence of the KWS over working with local people has undermined its own community-based conservation efforts. 'Professor' Nkutai's story illustrates how, despite initiatives undertaken by Maasai to protect wildlife, the community commitment has been weakened by government ambivalence over the recognition of community efforts.

Although communities are protecting wildlife, Maasai land owners are committing few resources to sustainable land management; they are mining the resource, but reinvesting little. The belief that once people benefit from wildlife they will act to sustain it appears to be only partially true. Income from tourism is often used to buy more livestock, which ironically may mean increased pressure on the land.

According to Nashuu, teaching people to invest in conservation rather than in social activities or increasing their herds was probably one of the biggest challenges facing community conservation. 'People are not ploughing back what they reap from wildlife. Communities must grapple with the fact that they have limited resources, and must learn to manage this sustainably. It is our responsibility as conservation agencies to help land owners find sustainable management systems to achieve their goals for a better life.'

We nevertheless came away with a feeling of hope, having learnt that wildlife has become an integral part of the Maasai economy and remains a proud heritage. During our journey we were constantly reminded of the continuing cohabitation between the Maasai and wildlife. Both positive and negative consequences of this close association were evident. The milk of this herd is not entirely drunk with honey; a bitter taste remains for some.

Milking the wild herd has therefore brought with it costs and conditions that are having a major impact on social structures and relationships as well as on wildlife and its environment. The Maasai have had to adapt to new demands in order to milk this herd. The shift from milk to money has introduced a new commodity with no customary system to guide and monitor its distribution and use. Milk production has taken on different forms – campsites, cultural bomas, handicrafts, concessions to tour companies – which require entirely new management institutions and skills.

Those who hold the gourd and distribute the milk are now representative committees and associations with youths and women as members, rather than the age group structures dominated by the male elders. Leaders are elected rather than selected, which has the potential to weaken the

fledgeling institutions managing wildlife and public money. Formal rather than traditional education provides youths with knowledge and skills, but overlooks ancient resource management knowledge, while introducing new values and aspirations which can pit individual ambition against communal welfare.

For a glimpse into the future we listened to Nashuu, a man with a foot in two worlds: the Maasai community and the KWS, the national body responsible for wildlife conservation. His story illustrates how the future of wildlife and the Maasai lies in the integration of knowledge and wisdom from both those worlds. Kenneth spent four years as a Maasai *moran* (warrior), a critical education in environment, social values and organisation. He had the foresight to see that Maasai future lay beyond pastoralism. He completed his schooling and found a job, but quit and returned home. There, as a conservation action leader, he began to educate and organise his people to fight for their rights to wildlife. He

was then taken on by KWS to pioneer extension work around Amboseli, and today he is responsible for KWS partnership activities in Narok District, which includes working with communities around the Maasai Mara Reserve. He says: 'It was incredible to have a young Maasai like me in this field, as our indigenous knowledge covers both livestock and wildlife. It has been an interesting adventure for me, as it would for any Maasai, as we are used to this work. Such experience has really built me up and motivated me to work in wildlife conservation.'

It is via people such as Nashuu that the chasm between ancient and modern could be bridged, allowing indigenous communities to prosper from resources on their land and regain their wholeness.

As Mokompo ole Simel had stated: 'Ore iltunganak ootumuta ingwesi neme sinyat' (People who have destroyed all their wildlife and live without it are not complete).

'In our original home, Masoka, we taught young boys how to trap animals, to make guns for the hunt, to weave fish traps, to understand the language of the forest, to respect every wild animal or bird, to live together with the animals. But today things have changed. We have to send them to school to learn other skills, new skills for a new life.'

Chief Cosmas Kanyurira, Masoka (Zimbabwe)

Zimbabwe

People and animals, a tense harmony

By Chenjerai Hove

Chiro, or 'the abode of baboons', in Zimbabwe's Gonarezhou National Park has been turned into an abode for tourists. But the original inhabitants of this site, a strategic one on the River Save, refuse to move. The people sleep in double beds with bedside lights and telephones; the baboons sleep in trees overhanging the deep pools, barking in the middle of the night and frightening the visitors. The baboons demand their place back; humans demand their new colony. The tension is there, visibly dramatised.

Gonarezhou lies in southern Zimbabwe, where it borders on South Africa and Mozambique. It means 'the abode of the elephant', and indeed the elephants in these parts are at home and agitated about it. They have been hunted and hounded during Zimbabwe's liberation war of the 1970s, and Mozambique's civil war of the 1970s and 1980s. So the elephants are vicious, not as calm as their brothers and sisters in Hwange game park in the south west which have never been subjected to the vagaries of human folly.

Until 1968 humans and animals lived together in this vast expanse of forests and watering points. It was the home of the animals as well as the Chauke, Mahenye, Chitsa, Tsvovani, and many others. Everyone respected everyone else's physical and spiritual space.

But in that year, when the Department of Parks and Wildlife took control of the park, the Chauke, Mahenye and others were forcibly removed, leaving their old homesteads to collapse and the graves of their ancestors to disappear in the jungles and thickets. They left behind the trees, hills, rivers and animals which were part of their history and world view. Shrines of hundreds of years were also left in solitude. The park became the sanctuary of elephants, lions, birds, baboons, kudu, eland, impala, birds and butterflies.

The Mahenye now occupy a small strip of land to the north of the park along the River Save. Every day they gaze across the river as if to say: those are the lands of our ancestors where we lived and shared life with the animals, birds, trees, and soils of the land. The earth gave in plenty. People and the animals received and enjoyed the gifts of nature, each according to their needs, since they had reached the silent accord which said that all children of nature are doomed to live together until the end of time.

Thus the mighty and gentle River Save is the new border between the animals and the people. Both drink from the cool waters of the river as it flows down to the ocean. Wild animals come to drink here, in the dark-green foliage. The people drink here too, but they want to fish and swim as they had done decades before the artificial partition, withdrawing when the time for wild animals to come and drink drew near.

Unfortunately, the animals know no boundaries. They cross over to hunt and graze, devouring the crops and the domestic animals of the people across the river, where the grass always seems greener. Humans too wish they had the same leeway as the wild animals, to cross each other's paths as they had done for so many years.

So the Mahenye look across the sands and waters of the River Save in envy. Their lands are now foreign soil to them. If they want to visit the graves of their ancestors, they have to obtain written permission from the Department of Parks and Wildlife Management, and if they want to bury their royalty in the park, as is the custom, they have to obtain written permission too. Even herbalists have to obtain permission to search for traditional herbs in the park.

'I was only four years when we were forced to move from our ancestral lands... but everyone wants to go back there,' says Cephas Chauke, son of Chief Mahenye. He talks of the excitement of

---

Shiri yakanaka unoindepi?
Shiri yakanaka unoindepi?
Huya huya tibhururuke!
Huya huya tibhururuke!
Takananga Kumakore!
Takananga kumakore!

(Beautiful bird, where are you flying to?
Beautiful bird
Where are you flying to?
Come, come,
Let's fly together!
Come, come
Let's fly together,
Heading for the clouds!
Heading for the clouds!)

A traditional children's song

---

the landscape which shaped his early childhood when he was learning to name things: the fat baobab trees, the ugly and vicious baboons, the clumsy elephants, the fearsome lions roaring every night for territorial dominance, and the stealthy leopards. Like many Mahenye people, Cephas – who works as a waiter – still clings to the memory of that life which is as far away from his current reality as the feather clouds hanging in the sky.

The tension between the park and the people is persistent. The people know the park does not belong to animals alone – it also belongs to them. They are entitled to live there and dream their dreams together with their animals. 'If they could speak our language, the animals would also say, "They are our people",' the Mahenye say.

Tourists came and hunted for sport, killing elephants, buffalo, kudu and many other animals and leaving the carcasses to be eaten by hyenas and jackals, or to rot in the park.

The people saw this with disbelief. Their ancestors had taught them to kill only what they could eat, sharing it with their families and neighbours. Never be so cruel as to kill an animal which has not invaded your crops or killed your domestic animals, the rule went. If one killed animals recklessly, it defiled the soil of the ancestors.

'We cannot understand it when strangers come to hunt the wild animals,' says Baba Sithole, a Mahenye elder; 'killing many elephants and leaving the carcasses to rot and decay. They take the horns and the skins, leaving the meat to rot. We just cannot understand it.'

Shadrack was a local boy with relatives in Mozambique and Zimbabwe; like the rest of the people in Mahenye, he knew no border between the two countries. (It must be said that the border here is nothing more than a concrete slab with sr, for Southern Rhodesia, on the one side, and pea, for Portuguese East Africa, on the other.

It is entirely unguarded, and the stream here is not big enough to stop a goat from crossing either way.)

Shadrack fought with FRELIMO in the then Mocambique in the 1960s and 1970s, and could also have fought with ZANLA in what was then Rhodesia, but by 1975 he was tired of war. He walked away with his guns and military skills and brought them to Mahenye.

Shadrack vowed never to let his people go hungry for meat when it was so abundant across the river, in the lands of their ancestors. So he took his guns and walked across the river, with the dark night and his ancestors protecting him. After the hunt he would walk back to the Mahenye and invite them into the park to collect the meat under cover of darkness.

For many years Shadrack hunted in the Gonarezhou, evading the gamekeepers. He hunted elephants for their ivory, and rhino for their horn. All the time he gave meat to the people. He drove a white Mercedes which he drove to Mahenye and hid with the help of the locals.

He hunted at night and slept during the day. He even opened a secret office, known as 'Shadrack's office', in the park itself. The office was in a massive baobab tree which was hollow inside. In earlier years, people had used the hollow baobab to hide from wild animals when night caught up with them before they got home. If lions challenged them, they hid in the tree. It was a shrine where sacrifices were offered to the ancestors.

So the elders told Shadrack about the hollow tree, and he camped there with a folding bed, chairs, paraffin stove, and some provisions. Nobody ever gave the secret away.

The villagers knew where he was, but would not tell; he was their silence and their secret. Local people were fond of him. After all, he was the first local to drive a Mercedes in style, like a government minister, with proceeds from the lands of his ancestors.

Then one day Shadrack's paraffin stove ran out of fuel, and he made a fire inside the boabab so that he could cook his afternoon meal. An alert game warder saw the smoke, and Shadrack

was captured. But since he had no guns, ivory or rhino horn with him, he could only be charged with loitering in the park without written permission. Eventually he only spent a few weeks in jail, and he was back in Mahenye, showing that he could beat the system.

Again they caught him, not in his abandoned office but sleeping under a tree with a gun for his pillow. This time he was convicted of loitering in the park and possession of an illegal weapon. This time, he spent a few months in jail.

The stories become varied at this point. Some say Shadrack is farming in Mozambique; others say he is working on a farm at Mazoe. All they know is that Shadrack's story belongs to both Zimbabwe and Mozambique, and for all one cares he might be an important person in either of those countries, retired from hunting and the regional wars which never seem to end.

'Shadrack was good with people, but bad with animals,' says Chauke, with a smile on his narrow face.

In the late 1980s the Department of Parks and Wildlife Management had an idea. If the likes of Shadrack had to be stopped from having their say about animals, the community had to be involved somehow. Ideas were tossed around, and much thinking went into it. If it was acknowledged that the community owned the animals, the new thinking went, then the community could help to preserve them.

Clive Stockill came by, speaking fluent Shona, Ndebele, Shangaan and English. His family had settled in the Chiredzi area decades before. Some were missionaries, and others were farmers. They have vast tracts of land in the area; cattle, eland, impalas, wild pigs, buffalo and birds all overflow on the Stockill farms.

Stockill talked with the villagers about how they could harness the animals for their own communal and personal use. The animals did not belong to the government, he declared; they belonged to the villagers.

So the latter took up the idea. They discussed ways of conserving wild animals in the olden days. They discussed the problem of game parks. Then things went into motion. Everyone wanted to conserve animals, for the sake of their children

and the survival of their communities as it had been before the coming of the white man.

That is the story of how Campfire (or the Communal Areas Management Programme of Indigenous Resources) came to Mahenye, to be embraced by the locals as their own dream of how modern game parks can merge with traditional knowledge of how humans can interact with animals for the benefit of both.

In time, the villagers put together a conservation plan covering every aspect of natural life, including human beings. Today the grass is tall and thick. The trees are not unnecessarily cut, and the fish are not fished at all. Grandparents no longer teach their grandchildren traditional methods of fishing and hunting.

Besides this, the Mahenye community harvests the animals for its own use. Tourists are allowed to hunt a certain number of animals, and the community also has an allocation. Revenue goes to community projects, and small amounts to households.

Until now the community has gained a school, clinic, borehole, and electric grinding mill, a watering point for domestic animals, and a traditional village. Plans for a community-run game park are far advanced. The hotel chain also donates a certain percentage of its earnings to

---

Simango was born in Gona reZhou, among the animals. Now he sits by his barren hut with a sooty roof. He is eating groundnuts without showing an appetite for the meal. Yesterday, an elephant came to his fields and ate his maize. He is dejected.
His wife and children can afford a smile for the visitors. But it is only an African smile, which tell the visitor that, even in our sorry state, we welcome you. Simango does not want to talk much. His heart is heavy.
'How can we have fat elephants which eat my maize, and I have thin children whose maize has been eaten by the animals? What is the use of having fat elephants and thin human beings?'

community projects. Add local employment to that, and the local people are happy that at least someone has come to acknowledge that the locals are part of the local nature scene, in a tense harmony which tourists come to see.

Campfire is also seen by many local people as a genuine attempt to restore the traditional respect and harmony between humans and other aspects of nature.

'*Kunzi munhu vanwe,*' the traditional saying goes – to be a dignified human being is to be acknowledged by others. The 'others' did not just mean other humans – it meant all other aspects of life. For, traditionally, everything was spiritual and holy. The river was holy. The hill next to your home was holy, the abode of the ancestors. You should not defile the land, ancestors decreed.

Campfire seemed to fit into the traditional philosophy of the local people, and it still does to a certain extent.

You arrive in Masoka, tired after a journey of nearly 500 kilometres from the capital, Harare. The road is rough, and red dust chokes people and machines. As soon as you enter the Masoka communal area, the road is dotted with patches of elephant dung, and sometimes lion footprints. The soil is untouched. The massive trees are interwoven with each other, forming an intricate pattern reminiscent of the relationship between all aspects of nature in these parts.

People, wild animals, trees and the soil are in some form of complex balance only the inhabitants know how to name. There are traditional laws that cement the relationship between people, animals, trees, the soil, and God.

As soon as you arrive, your first port of call is the village leader. You pay him a token sum, but he immediately announces that it is not for him; he will take it to the spiritual leader, Nyamasoka, to inform him that there are strangers in the village, intending to interact with the local people.

The spiritual leader tells the chief that the strangers are not people of bad intent, and should be assisted to learn what they want. (Should he say no, the strangers would be asked to leave.)

'But we are a people who give generosity first to strangers and then to ourselves,' says Chief Cosmas Kanyurira, after the strangers are at home in the village.

'You shall not kill what you cannot eat,' one commandment says. Another states: 'Respect the

---

'*A professional hunter was told not to disturb the dogs of the wild (lions), and particularly never to fire guns at them. But one day, in the early evening, the dogs of the wild chased a water buck into the hunter's camp. He fired a shot into the air, and the lions ran away.*

'*The next morning the spiritual leader sent the chief to find out from the hunter why a shot had been fired the previous evening. The hunter denied that he had fired a gun at all.*

'*"You know the rules of our ancestors," the chief said. "If you are lying, do not go hunting for the next seven days."*

'*Since the hunter did not believe such superstitions, he took a client out to hunt the following day. The client wanted to kill a buffalo bull.*

'*As soon as they left the camp, they saw a bull standing in the open, gazing at the vehicle. The client wounded the bull; drowning in pain, it ran into a nearby thicket. The men had to track it; never leave an injured buffalo in the bush, the law said, as that is death for the passer-by. Suddenly, the bull charged and ripped open the client's belly. The client tried to run, but the bull gored him to death before the guides could shoot it.*

'*In the afternoon the hunter brought the news to the headman, who took the message to Nyamasoka. He confessed that they had fired the shots the previous night.*

'*Our ancestors left us certain rules about how to live together with wild animals.*'

Chief Cosmas Kanyurira, Masoka Communal Lands

soil, because it gives you food and is also the abode of your ancestors.' And a third: 'Do not kill the dogs of the wild (lions) unless they have attacked people or domestic animals.'

It is mid-April, and the people of Masoka are harvesting. The harvest is a dual one. The people grow maize, cotton, sorghum, pumpkins and watermelons. During the day men, women and children work in the fields enveloped by tall trees and green grass with blades as sharp as razors. The surrounding forests are undisturbed and impenetrable. In there lies another harvest: wild animals, that live off each other as well as on the people who wish to eat their meat. A delicate balance has been created between the life of wild animals and the life of the villagers. This is a world of shared spaces.

Nobody dares to venture into the thick forests that wall up the narrow footpaths and hunters' makeshift roads. But there are other footpaths too that break the dense undergrowth. Daylight belongs to the people in their fields and homes.

'We were moved from our original homes. They asked us to move, because they said the place was now reserved for animals. We settled here, and some of us went to Angwa. Some people refused to move; they said, no, we cannot move, this is our place. We moved from the original Masoka to this place, called Mazunga. We had to walk through the forest; there were no roads, no vehicles, nothing to carry our property to this new place. They even burnt some of the houses, especially in 1975 when we had to move again because of the liberation war. Trucks came to take our household goods to the "keeps" (protected villages). After the war, we came back. Some went back to the original Masoka, but they were not allowed to settle there. We love the original Masoka. The soil is rich there; it is the home of our ancestors.
'We would love to go back to our original home. But the Parks people will arrest us if they find us, even if you say to them, "I am coming to see the grave of my father or the other ancestors".'
Mai Mhofu, an elderly woman and conservation leader in Masoka.

Mauya vadzimba
Maita, Samanyanga
Maita, sango rinopa aneta
Hekanhi Samanyanga
Tikafira pano wani.

(Thank you, blessed hunter
Thank you, wielder of large horns
Thank you, forests reward those who persist
We thank you Samanyanga [elephant]
We live here till we die.)
Praise poem for Chief Kanyurira after a successful
hunt.

The night belongs to the owners of the
underworld of dense forest foliage. Elephants,
buffalo, kudu, waterbuck, eland, zebras … name
them and they are there, roaming the wild,
sharing space with humans, forest and insects.
'You see the maize in the field over there? We
harvest during the day, but the animals harvest at
night,' says chief Kanyurira, with a rueful smile
on his white-bearded face. He laughs at the drama
in which man and animal share the same arena.

Fences, fences, fences. Arrival in Masoka begins
with a drive or walk along an electric fence. The
community has bought a solar panel, not to light
their homes but to electrify the fence around
their 18 square kilometres of communal land.

The current is supposed to be strong enough to
repel the animals. But no, the night is forever
being disturbed by the gong-gong of tins and
screaming human voices, trying to frighten
buffalo and elephants. The fence works for
elephants when they try to pull it down with their
long hands (trunks); the shock sends them back to
the reserve, where they should reside. But their
friends, the buffalo, are stubborn; they charge
from a distance and break the fence before they
feel the shock. In seconds they are flooding the
fields, devouring the dry maize cobs and cotton
stalks. Next, they trample the cotton plants to the
ground.

Yes, there are buffalo herds at Masoka that number more than 1 000 each – 1 000 angry buffalo which don't care a hoot how many tins people bang at once in the middle of the night. They stand there in the fields, chewing the maize and the cotton stalks, unperturbed. Even guns being fired into the air is mere entertainment; they seem to know the people of Masoka are not allowed to shoot them, and neither are the local game scouts.

But it is harvest time for the people of Masoka as well as the animals. 'We now preserve them so we can harvest them', says Chief Kanyurira. He explains that the community is selling hunting concessions to professional hunters who bring rich tourists to hunt in the area. An elephant costs up to $10 000, a buffalo and lion $5 000, and so on. The people of Masoka have also negotiated a quota to be killed for themselves.

The hunting revenue is used for development; thus far the community has gained a clinic, a school, the electric fence, community offices, grain storage rooms and two tractors, and new road-building projects are being planned.

'We have a new arrangement now. No, we cannot kill wild animals. They help us grow in a different way. From selling them we can do many things which were not possible before. The school there, the clinic, the storage house; it is because of the animals.' – *Mai Mhofu*

The tractors have been bought to plough the fields, since local people cannot own cattle or donkeys. Tsetse flies swarm the air like butterflies, and any cow that dares walk on the Masoka dust dies in hours. Donkeys have no chance either; goats, however, survive.

As the sun sets, the chief stares at his small patch of dry maize stalks. He knows he wants them, but he also knows the buffalo and the elephant behind the hot fence want to fill their mouths with his crop.

In earlier years the wild animals also ate the crops – but the people hunted the animals, killed some and ate them. Men, women and children celebrated the success of the hunt. When the desire for meat assailed their palates, they grouped and allowed themselves to be engulfed by the forests in search of their friends, the wild animals. The hunters carried *magidi* (home-made guns); nobody stopped them.

Today, however, these hunting traditions and skills are vanishing. Children are no longer taught the survival skills of making guns, snares, and *madhibhuras* (animal traps). When the professional hunters kill an elephant they take the tusks and skin and give the meat to the villagers. So the villagers, despite knowing where the animals hide in the forests, wait for meat to be delivered to them by those who hunt for sport.

'They shoot the buffalo across the fence. The buffalo escape into the fields where they are not shot. We cannot trap them. Our fields are places of shame; we feel ashamed when we walk in our fields, destroyed by buffalo. – *Woman, Masoka*

We are waiting for the hunter, his game scouts and trackers. 'He will be coming soon; his client has killed a bull elephant,' the excited workers in green uniforms tell us. Soon we hear the sound of a four-wheel-drive vehicle, and then another. We walk to the platform where many carcasses have been off-loaded.

The people of Masoka once celebrated this triumphant return from the hunt with a praise song to the *vadzimba* (heroes of the hunt). Then, the hunters arrived under cover of the night. Their wives softly sang to the hunters and ancestors, and wiped the men's heads with a cloth and love.

The professional hunter also arrives at night, relieved that none of his clients had been gored by a buffalo. The people of Masoka, Ward 11, wait. Today, their *vadzimba* is the safari operator. Times have changed; the former hunters are mere recipients of cut pieces of meat instead of 'givers' of whole carcasses. Their pride has been sacrificed on the altar of progress.

The morning will see the arrival of yet another carcass, this time an elephant. The day before yesterday it was a buffalo. The tired faces of the scouts and trackers show it has been a tiring and trying day.

'In our original home, Masoka, we taught young boys how to trap animals, to make guns for the hunt, to weave fish traps, to understand the language of the forest, to respect every wild animal or bird, to live together with the animals. But today things have changed. We have to send them to school to learn other skills – new skills for a new life.' – *Chief Cosmas Kanyurira*

The professional hunter also has his problems and concerns. Young married couples, he says, seek more and more land on which to settle and cultivate cotton, maize, pumpkins and sorghum. The more humans increase, the more the land for animals shrinks.

In the meantime, though, it's another day, another elephant, another lion, another happy

---

'I went fishing with my friend once. Fishing is in my blood. If I do not fish I will die. My father was a fisherman. His father too was a fisherman.
'But one day as I prepared to set my fishing lines, a buffalo was hiding in the thickets. It charged and got me. You see the wound, it broke a few of my ribs. I was lucky I had a strong belt for my pants. The horns of the buffalo bull hooked onto my belt. It dangled me for a while, and when I dropped, the buffalo was confused. It ran away. My friend shouted to the village for help. I survived, and I still fish. I am not angry against a buffalo. Maybe I had disturbed it.'
Baba Hwani

foreign client who has successfully killed a 'bull', if the hunter has irony enough to see the farce in hunting for sport.

Be that as it may, the people of Masoka have found an intricate balance between traditional and modern ways of conserving animals and other aspects of nature. Their dos and don'ts are so many that if a hunter arrives, they ensure that they assign a local person to him to ensure that no rules of the wild are broken. Thou shall not! Thou shall not!

Thus a new, tense harmony has been established between humans and animals, creating a new ecosystem and balance of nature which is sometimes difficult to understand. The Masoka people know that for the past 30 years no one there has been killed by a lion. The Mahenye people also know that, within living memory, no one has been killed by lions or other wild animals without their peace having been unnecessarily disturbed. Anyone who dares go into the private space of animals and people becomes a victim of his or her own folly.

The philosophy of the villagers is that everything – birds, animals, trees, insects, soils, and the sky – is part of nature. It is as if every living thing is there because of every living thing, a balanced dependency that respects the ecosystem as advised by the ancestors and still to be given to the children. And whoever dares to disturb that eco-balance faces the wrath of all aspects of nature.

'Previously, I never thought about wildlife and its links to tourism. On the farm we were against elephants – they drank your water and destroyed your garden. Like most people then, I felt someone should come and take these creatures away.'

Paula Adams, Kunene region (Namibia)

Namibia's Kunene region

A new vision unfolds

By Margaret Jacobsohn

'Start your farming with people…'
Part of an old Himba/Herero proverb

The spectacular landscapes of north-western Namibia mean different things to different people. Many tourists, seeking out the 'healing wilderness' as an antidote to crowded and polluted cities, are awed and uplifted by these rugged moonscapes. Others are appalled by the heat and isolation, and wonder how the 80 000 residents of the Kunene region survive.

For the people who live in the north west, who have to make a living from the land, the economic options *are* limited, although – contrary to popular belief – a lack of water is not their major problem. Domestic stock and wildlife die of starvation, not of thirst, in the regular cycles of drought experienced in the area. Nevertheless, most people are subsistence farmers, relying mainly on stock, with small-scale gardens where water – and marauding elephants and other wildlife – allow.

Kunene residents are culturally diverse: semi-nomadic Himba cattle herders, more sedentary Herero pastoralists, Damara stock farmers, a few Nama families, and the Roman Catholic Riemvasmaak farming community. Although the most 'traditional' of these groups, the Himba are among the wealthiest cattle herders in Africa and must rank among the most successful of Namibia's subsistence farmers. But most people, the Himba included, have aspirations – at least

for their children, if not for themselves – that cannot be met by a subsistence economy. Younger people want cash for clothes, radios, cars – and this means jobs.

Government, tourism and conservation NGOs are the major employers in the region, offering no more than a thousand or so jobs between them. Distance from the capital and from markets, limited as the latter are in vast Namibia with its low population, means that development choices are restricted.

Nevertheless, in a bold legislative reform initiative the Namibian government has opened a range of new opportunities to remote area dwellers in Kunene, Caprivi, and elsewhere. In this journey into the north west, six rural Namibians who have grasped the opportunities offered by the 1996 amendments to Namibia's conservation laws share with us their relationship with their land, and their hopes for the future.

Although the legislation devolves conditional rights over wildlife and tourism to communal area dwellers, thus giving them the same conditional rights enjoyed by owners of freehold land, its effect has been to bring some people back to the land. For many it has changed their relationship with the natural environment, and deepened their sense of place.

Wildlife has once again become relevant to communal area dwellers, as an economic and spiritual resource. The so-called communal area conservancy legislation gives communities a legal mechanism for taking responsibility for wildlife back from the government. Accordingly, communities now feel accountable for their wildlife instead of being alienated from a resource that was previously the sole responsibility of the state.

Communal area conservancies centre on a deceptively simple concept: giving a self-defined group of farmers living on communal or state land – which is the status of most Namibian land – the right to register a certain area as a conservancy. A conservancy is a clearly defined but fenceless multiple-use zone supporting farming, wildlife and tourism, plus any other activity residents wish to introduce. A number of legal conditions, aimed at ensuring a democratic process, must be met before the government will register the conservancy, thus giving members of the conservancy legal rights over wildlife and tourism in the area.

The concept is simple, but in fact involves a paradigm shift in both conservation and rural development. Firstly, it sees wildlife as the valuable African resource it is, and provides a way for this resource to be incorporated into the local economy. This diversifies rural economies and allows African people to find their own alternative routes to development instead of slavishly following Eurocentric models that have mostly failed in Africa, vast amounts of 'development aid' notwithstanding.

The conservancy legislation facilitates a democratic process and operates as an enabling structure which does not rigidly dictate exactly how different rural communities will integrate conservancies into their local economies. A semi-nomadic Himba community, skilled at common property management via a descent-based lineage leadership structure, may end up running its conservancy very differently from the way in which a group of sedentary Damara farmers, with a well-developed farmers' union, may operate theirs.

Mindful that in too many instances in post-colonial Africa the rich have got richer and the

poor poorer, the Namibian government sees the role of the conservancy as uplifting the community as a whole. This is where the enabling legislation has been particularly creative, combining free enterprise with common property management.

Faced with the gross inequalities of land distribution inherited from the colonial regime – and the reality that there is simply not enough arable land in Namibia to enable each family in a communal area to own a private farm – the government envisages communal area conservancies as one of the ways in which remote area dwellers can supplement their farming activities. Wildlife thus becomes a primary resource for a conservancy hoping to attract eco-tourists, and with wise management a conservancy can become a centre of development in a remote rural area, attracting investment and stimulating jobs and income for its members.

The conservancy does not stifle free enterprise, as individuals are encouraged to start tourism-related businesses. However, as such businesses are based on a common resource – wildlife – and use communally owned land, the entrepreneur, whether local or not, is required by law to enter into a contract with the local conservancy committee. The details of such a contract is left to the two parties; it could range from a joint venture with the conservancy, or it could merely require the enterprise to pay a small bed-night levy, or employ and train a minimum number of local people. A key player here has been the Legal Assistance Centre, an NGO of lawyers, formerly anti-apartheid activists, who now represent the legal interests of communal area conservancies.

As the law requires the conservancy committee to be a democratically elected body, members and office bearers are voted on to it by the conservancy members. Conservancy leaders are thus held locally accountable for their decisions and actions. A committee that consistently acts against its members' wishes or is deemed to be corrupt can be constitutionally deposed.

An equitable benefit distribution plan which must be ratified by the membership and can be regularly updated, ensures that members have a democratic input into how income to the conservancy is used and distributed. Eventually, a conservancy should become independent of start-up donor aid and earn sufficient income to survive as a profitable enterprise, owned by its members. By late 1999 one communal area conservancy was already paying 80 per cent of its own running costs, and had N$300 000 in the bank. It intends to be fully independent by end 2000.

The legislation has been misunderstood – perhaps wilfully – by some local and outside entrepreneurs. These include people who would prefer the free-for-all land grab that prevailed at independence to continue. Some tour operators – and some local entrepreneurs – fear losing their freedom to do as they wish in communal areas. Now that communal area dwellers have a mechanism with which to organise themselves, tour operators will no longer be able to treat remote communal areas as their private playgrounds. What they will get instead, by entering into a structured and formal relationship with a conservancy committee, is security of tenure, an organised body through which they can communicate with local people, and a protected natural environment including wildlife.

The six people given voice here could not be more different; they are a young, feisty women's rights activist, a middle-aged farmer and family head, a professional tourist guide, a young man working in wildlife conservation, a Himba great-grandmother and trance healer, and a Herero sub-elder. What they share is a vision for their communities that includes local empowerment, income, jobs, domestic stock, and wildlife in a healthy natural habitat.

But the vision does not stop here. In the long run, local people will assume a leading role in managing their own water, forest and other plant resources, with the government providing technical input and services as required and co-ordinated by conservancy members. Thus conservancies enable their members to manage their own environments. It is this local element that has so often been missing in past rural development and conservation initiatives. As the old Himba proverb says, 'start your farming with people, not with cattle'.

PAULA ADAMS, 30, SINGLE PARENT, COMMUNITY DEVELOPMENT ACTIVATOR, EMPLOYED BY THE TORRA CONSERVANCY

Paula's story could have been very different: Sitting at her desk in the Torra Conservancy office, she laughs when she thinks of how amazed her teachers from her troubled, rebellious schooldays would be to see her today, playing a positive leadership role in her rural community.

'I have now found a purpose in life,' says this small, determined woman neatly dressed in khaki. That she loves her job – which weds her passion for women's rights to the opportunity to be a catalyst for grass roots development – is obvious. 'My key role,' she adds, 'is to make sure that women in my community have a voice – that they get information about the conservancy, and that they have the opportunity to make their input.'

Has she seen a difference in women's involvement in the five years she has worked here? 'Very definitely. Women used to be spectators, watching men take part in meetings. Now we are all players, women and men.' In fact, she says, tongue in cheek, she does not discriminate between the genders in disseminating information; 'I work equally with men and women.'

Another big change she has witnessed is a more positive attitude among local people to wildlife, including elephants. Paula includes herself in this attitude shift. 'Previously, I never thought about wildlife and its links to tourism. On the farm we were against elephants – they drank your water and destroyed your garden. Like most people then, I felt someone should come and take these creatures away.

'Now I know people and wildlife can live together. Yes, our elephants can cause problems, but they and other wildlife also bring benefits.'

Such benefits include money. At the time of the interview, Torra Conservancy had more than N$300 000 in the bank. This sum had been derived from two sources: members' annual payout from their joint tourism venture, the luxury tented Damaraland Camp; and the proceeds of the conservancy's first annual trophy hunting contract. This income is likely to rise to well over N$1million a year within the next few years as a second tourism joint venture and other related enterprises get under way.

As secretary of the conservancy committee, as well as the conservancy's CDA, Paula attended a training workshop for conservancy committees on equitable benefit distribution. The committee then drew up a plan which is being ratified by members.

After covering the running costs of the conservancy, the committee hopes to address the need for local jobs by initiating several development projects, such as a campsite with a walking trail, staffed by local unemployed youths. An education fund enabling academically gifted children to study further is another part of the plan, as is an environmental 'crisis fund'. This will help alleviate the financial need of members in emergencies such as drought.

We recall how an elephant killed a local man who was walking home at night a few years ago.

'There was no conservancy at that time, so there was no help for the family except from individuals,' Paula observes. 'Today we would be able to use conservancy funds to cover funeral costs, and if a breadwinner was killed we would be able to assist the family financially for a few months.'

Paula was born and spent the first two of her 30 years at Riemvasmaak on the Orange River in northern South Africa. In 1971, in what was arguably one of the most iniquitous 'Group Areas removals' by the former South African regime, the community was brutally uprooted from its riverside farmlands and trucked to northern Namibia, more than 3 000 kilometres away. Families were resettled on farms formerly owned by whites in the arid western strip of 'new Damaraland', one of a patchwork of 'homelands' for different population groups created in terms of apartheid ideology.

Even though her parents, her grandmother and two aunts went 'home', Paula chose not to return to the new South Africa when Riemvasmakers were given the opportunity to do so a few years ago.

Although she misses her parents 'every day', she has no ambivalence about staying behind in Namibia: 'This is my home, the place where I grew up,' she exclaims. Paula gestures towards the red and brown vista beyond the office windows: ancient fields of basalt, or volcanic lava, eroded into innumerable autumn-shaded rocks; gravel plains; small wedges of green vegetation; a few small trees … The sense of wide open space is emphasised rather than broken by the nearby and distant rock-capped hills, characteristically flat-topped or breast-shaped.

Torra's small but handsome three-roomed office blends into this landscape, having been built from local stone by a team led by a talented local builder, Marcus Roman. The office, on the main road north, is opposite the school at Bergsig, Torra's only 'town'. Two shops, a clinic, the school buildings, a hostel, teachers' houses and a score or so other homesteads are the sum total of the settlement.

Since the conservancy office was built in 1998 a new shop has been erected alongside it by a local schoolteacher/businessman, hoping to attract the tourists who often stop at the conservancy office for information. A sign in the shop cannily offers conservancy members a discount on their purchases.

Paula's schooling at Arandis near Swakopmund about 400 kilometres to the south was interrupted by the birth of the first of her two children. Although as a 16-year-old unwed mother she insisted on returning to school to finish the interrupted year, her schooldays were over.

A few years later economic imperatives and single parenthood forced her home to her family's farm, Betanie. But she did not enjoy the life. Her routine of housework, cooking and looking after kid goats, with only the radio for entertainment, was dull and boring for a young woman accustomed to television, karate classes, and a lively social life. And so she drifted towards the nearest bright lights, relatively speaking: the town of Khorixas.

Here, in her early 20s, she started developing a social conscience and also a sense of initiative. Encountering numerous abused women, Paula and a small group of women decided to do something about it. With no resources beyond energy and a sense of injustice, they launched a women's organisation, Ma/hao, meaning 'stand together', against the abuse of women and children. They held workshops and mobilised other women; soon, the organisation was flourishing in this dusty frontier town. Ma /hao, now with an office, transport, and a portfolio of women's projects, is regarded as a fine example of what can be achieved by grass roots activism.

Paula would not have come home to Torra – and her community would have lost the skills and energy of an outstanding young person – were it not for the interesting job opportunities opening up within the then still developing conservancy.

Besides facilitating women's participation in conservation and development, the conservancy CDA runs the office, staffs the high-frequency radio, facilitates surveys, and organises and often leads meetings. The radio connects the office to the outside world, and facilitates local links via a line-of-sight network of five smaller radios. This means the office has become a key centre of communication at Bergsig, which is more than 100 kilometres from Khorixas.

'But this is not just a job to me,' says Paula; 'it's an opportunity to make a difference. The post has turned me into a leader. As such one attracts conflict, and I have had to learn to stay calm and become strong.'

One of her biggest challenges thus far was dealing with the professional hunter to whom the conservancy sold its small trophy hunting quota in 1999. The hunter was selected by the committee on the basis of his tender, but numerous operational issues needed to be thrashed out before and while he brought his clients into the area. This included labour issues, meat distribution, communication between the hunter and conservancy members, and so on.

The memory of some of their early clashes makes Paula grin: 'Ag, he is a nice man … but we had to find each other. On the one side you had a white hunter not used to a young black woman leading the discussions, and perhaps also not expecting such an organised, empowered community …' Diplomatically, Paula admits she also had much to learn in terms of communicating with the hunter.

She is openly proud at having successfully represented the conservancy committee and navigated some thorny patches. 'It was hard, but we got it right. I learned how to stand up for myself, and I think now we have mutual respect. If the same person wins the next contract, I will have no problems working with him.'

It's lunchtime, and Paula prepares to lock up the office and cross the road to her small, neat, reed and corrugated iron house with its white-painted door. Her father built the house for her before he went back to Riemvasmaak. Her last task before she locks the office is to check that the box of condoms, prominently marked 'Free: help yourself', that she keeps on a shelf for all takers is still full enough. Torra Conservancy may be aimed at diversifying the local economy to include wildlife and tourism, but the improved social organisation it has triggered off spills over into other areas – HIV/AIDS prevention included.

JAN RHYN, FARMER, FAMILY HEAD, TORRA CONSERVANCY
MEMBER

Oom Jan, as he is widely known, is the archetypal man of the land: tall, sinewy and wise, with a level gaze that belies his quick humour.

Although he spent many years working as a miner, farming has always been in his blood, and he knew he would return home one day to take charge of the family farm.

He greets us at the gate – bedecked with kudu horns – of the family homestead, Fonteine. Behind him are the clusters of masonry buildings and shacks that are home to different units of his extended family; dogs, in various shapes and sizes, lie in the shade, too hot to bark at visitors. The buildings are much repaired, and some have seen better days, but there is nothing ramshackle about this set-up – this is obviously a working farm.

On the southern horizon, in a purple haze, the spectacular Huab River valley is visible. Like all rivers running west, except for the Orange on Namibia's southern border with South Africa and the Kunene River on the Angolan border, the Huab is a desert or ephemeral river – one that flows for only a few hours or days each year if good rains fall in its catchment.

To the north, west and east of the farm are the gravel and red rock plains and hills of the southern Kunene region. A herd of goats winds its way home as the day wanes. Six springbok feed near them.

Oom Jan leads us to a shady courtyard at the back of the main house. He turns off the portable radio hooked to the courtyard wall, and sends children running to find more chairs. Having stood down in late 1999 as vice-chairman of Torra Conservancy, after serving in this position for several years, he feels well qualified to talk about community-based conservation and how it has changed people's relationship with the land. His election to the committee was not entirely welcome; as a busy farmer he was not sure he could spare the time, but the experience – and the opportunity to work for his community – is obviously something he has valued.

He is quick to point out that it is only in the past few years that he has seen any sense in wildlife conservation.

'Wildlife was not important to me previously. Lions and hyena ate our stock, and we just wanted to get rid of them. When the conservancy talk started, my reaction was, no man, here the elephants make themselves at home in our gardens. There should be *less* wildlife, not more … if wild animals increase out here, later we won't be able to farm.

'I went to the meetings and heard about the benefits wildlife could bring us. Then I would go home and struggle with the elephants destroying my garden. I thought conservancies were just a way to give wildlife our land.

'Then IRDNC [Integrated Rural Development and Nature Conservation, the local NGO] gave me the conservancy toolbox, and I sat down and read it.' The toolbox is a booklet produced by the Namibian Ministry of Environment and Tourism, outlining the implications of the changed legislation for communal farmers and listing the steps towards conservancy formation.

'As I read,' Oom Jan continues, 'it dawned on me that the conservancy plan was really no different from my plan on the farm – just bigger. My family and I try to farm so that we are as self-sufficient as possible. You look after your stock so that you can use it sustainably for your family. If we had rights over the wildlife, if we could sustainably use some of our springbok and gemsbok, it would be the same … from a farmer's point of view, the conservancy idea made great sense. Wildlife could help us *all* make a living; it could help stop our youths from disappearing into towns, because we could create jobs out here; it could bring us income.'

Income from wildlife became a reality for the people in the area even before the conservancy was registered in 1998 – thanks to the country's first joint tourism venture between a private company and a local community. As the nearest farmer to the proposed location of the joint venture, a luxury tented lodge, Oom Jan was directly involved from the start.

'When I first heard of the proposal in 1995, I was against it. To me it sounded like: today you build a lodge, tomorrow I have to move out … After all, it was my farming area they were proposing to use. Luckily, I did not close my mind to the idea, and on reflection I saw the possibility of work opportunities – not necessarily for me, but for my family and others in the community.'

The 'possibilities' foreseen by Oom Jan quickly translated into 12 permanent jobs for local people at the new Damaraland Camp, as well as temporary work for more people during its construction. The community share was about N$80 000 in the first year, N$120 000 in the second, and more than N$180 000 in 1999. As the camp grows in popularity, and occupancy rates increase, so this amount will increase. The young camp has already won two awards – the British Guild of Travel Writers has chosen it as one of the three best eco-tourism destinations in the world, and Namib Wilderness tourists have voted it the top venue out of eight. After 10 years, in 2007, the conservancy may exercise an option to take over the camp as its own business. This would be phased in over a further five years.

As the nearest neighbour, Oom Jan had to agree to share the farm's relatively plentiful water supply with the camp. The solar-powered pump used by the lodge now also serves the farm, and, as a line of sheets and towels on the washing line attests, women on the farm are earning good income running a laundry service.

Oom Jan takes us on a tour of the farmyard. Down a slope, past a small earth dam dug by him and his late father, he leads the way to his beloved garden, beleaguered by elephants, kudu, baboons and rabbits. When his family was resettled here from Riemvasmaak in 1973, he says, 'there was no garden and no fruit trees – just the house.'

The huge garden, a product of 26 years' work, would be noteworthy anywhere. In this environment it is a truly extraordinary achievement, a monument to hard work and determination. Its lush green shades in startling contrast with the predominantly red and brown backdrop, there are small orchards of fruit trees – orange, paw-paw, figs, bananas, dates; a neatly pruned vineyard; prickly pears; rows of sweet potatoes; beds of pumpkin, watermelon, spanspek (melon) and tomatoes; a field of mealies; lucerne for kid goats; elephant grass for the donkeys.

Literally tens of thousands of rocks and stones were moved by hand to clear the various plots; then donkeys were used to plough the unyielding soil. The plough still lies near the edge of the garden.

Oom Jan points to the orderly lines of young green mealies: 'The elephants are just waiting for those to ripen,' he jokes. In fact, he thinks he may have the edge on the elephants, at least for a while. As part of a 'problem animal' experiment by IRDNC, funded by the WWF and the British government, he has just erected a solar-powered electric fence around the garden. If experiences elsewhere are anything to go by, the fence will deter elephants for a year or two, and then they will learn ways to breach it. Wildlife problems are rarely solved – just alleviated.

As Oom Jan talks, he often uses the word 'team' – the team (of conservancy committee members) who negotiated with the professional hunter; the family team on the farm. This belief that if you work as a team you can move mountains (or, in his case, thousands of rocks), coupled with the tenet that if you want something you should go out and make it happen, sums up his life philosophy, he says.

As he walks us to our vehicle, he points out the herd of springbok that have followed the goats and are now grazing within 200 metres of the homestead: 'It's a wonderful thing to have wildlife on your land …' he muses. We drive away, leaving him in the amber glow of sunset, a farmer gazing with satisfaction over his land.

BONIFATIUS RUBEN/AWARAB, TOURIST GUIDE, TORRA CONSERVANCY CHAIRMAN AND FARMER

A tall and well-built 36-year-old, Bonifatius, or Boni, sits back in his chair and stretches his arms wide open to convey a point. He has the full attention of his listeners, six tourists grouped around a campfire, as he concludes his tale about the night lions got into his neighbour's sheep kraal.

The next morning he will lead the tourists on a walking tour, stopping to reveal the small and large miracles of life that are common in this arid and beautiful landscape. Although Boni is chairman of the Torra Conservancy, his job takes him out of the conservancy into a neighbouring tourism concession area run by Dennis Liebenberg, owner-manager of the small tented camp Etendeka.

Tourism was not a career Boni had envisaged for himself, largely because there was almost no tourism in what was then Damaraland when he grew up in the 1960s and 1970s. Born in the Ugab

River area of southern Kunene as one of a family of 10 children, he received most of his schooling at Roman Catholic mission schools. He drifted into a job at the Uis tin mine, where his father worked, and was training as a fitter when the mine closed down.

Boni then developed his creative talents and earned some money carving gravestones and doing wood carvings. But, as a married man with three children to support, he needed a job. When he heard that the newly built Etendeka Mountain Camp had an opening he cycled there on the rocky dirt track, a journey of several hours. The post was already taken, and he rode back jobless. But his marathon bike ride must have impressed Dennis Liebenberg, because the following year, in March 1995, Boni was hired as the camp guide.

Boni enjoys tourism, and sees himself opening his own camp one day. As a tourist guide he could immediately see the link between wildlife and tourism, and the need for benefits besides jobs to devolve down to the people who live with the wildlife. Etendeka was one of the first tourist camps in Namibia to pay an annual bed-night levy to neighbouring communities.

Boni was elected chairman of the Torra conservancy committee in 1997, and elected for a second two-year term in September 1999.

When he looks back at Torra's history, a number of highlights come to mind. 'Obviously, a great moment was our registration in 1998, after several years' hard work and community mobilisation. Credit must go to the vision of local leaders such as Bennie Roman, who did much of the work needed to get the project going. We have also had great support from the governor of Kunene, Simpson Tjongerero.

'Something else I'm very proud of is that we are the first of the communal area conservancies to cover our own running costs. So far we have reduced WWF donor funding by 80 per cent; in another year we will be 100 per cent self-sufficient.

'Assuming responsibility to run the conservancy is no small thing: it is a big business, and we must ensure that we manage it well. We can't waste resources that belong to the next generation.'

Another high point Boni wants to talk about is the two-week visit he and his committee undertook to study the Campfire programme in Zimbabwe. 'It was an invaluable experience for us all. Apart from seeing the similarities and differences between the two countries' conservation legislation at first hand, we learnt what it felt like to be tourists in a strange country. Many of us had never actually been tourists before, and the experience helped us understand tourism in the conservancy. We also developed a great team spirit. Travelling together taught us to accommodate different viewpoints as a committee.'

Something that particularly impressed Boni in Zimbabwe was the spirit of rural Zimbabweans. 'People do things for themselves; they don't sit back and wait for the government to do it for them. There's too much of that attitude here. Our government has given us the chance to go forward with the conservancy laws, and we must seize that opportunity.'

A priority for the conservancy committee in the future, according to Boni, is to continue working towards a common vision. 'We also need to use some of the funds we have in the conservancy bank account to start enterprises that create local jobs.'

Low points during his chairmanship include the theft of some of the trophy hunting meat from outside the Torra office which was intended for distribution among members. 'Although we have to blame ourselves for poor organisation, we need to react strongly against this theft of public property, and make sure it does not happen again.'

By now it is late, and the tourists have drifted off to bed. How does the chairman see the future? Boni picks up a piece of firewood and weighs it in his woodcarver's hands. 'We must not stop at sustainably managing our wildlife. We also need to be concerned about our trees, our wood. Conservancies are a way to organise ourselves to manage the future.'

VITALUS FLORRY, FIELD OFFICER, TORRA CONSERVANCY

Vitalus lives up to his name: at age 32 his vitality and enthusiasm for life express themselves in his speech and body language. He is one of those fortunate people who have found a way to combine what they love with earning a living.

The fourth child in a family of eight, he grew up within 30 kilometres of the Torra

Conservancy office. His education at a high school in Khorixas ended abruptly during his standard 8 year when a bottle thrown during a fight between others cost him the sight in one eye.

After medical treatment, Vitalus feared he had missed too much schooling to catch up. So he went home to the family farm and worked with the stock. Coming to terms with the loss of an eye was eased by the fact that his herding duties brought him into contact with the nature he had always loved.

'It was a time of great drought, and I had to move around a lot with the stock to find grazing. Predators were causing huge losses at the time, taking sheep and donkeys. I remember one night when our camp was surrounded by a pride of lions. We were all unarmed, and all we could do was throw bottles and rocks.'

Despite or perhaps because of such encounters, Vitalus's knowledge of and interest in the natural environment grew. When in 1993 his community sought to appoint four community game guards, his name was immediately put forward. He was promoted to field officer within two years, and

today leads a team of five game guards for Torra Conservancy.

His duties include organising and leading patrols, monitoring wildlife, writing and co-ordinating reports, paying salaries, conducting anti-poaching operations, liaising with Ministry of Environment and Tourism (MET) staff, guiding visitors and donors, giving feedback to the conservancy committee, and undertaking extension work with conservancy members and schoolchildren.

An aspect of his work he obviously finds exciting is the new wildlife monitoring system which he has helped to set up in the conservancy, in collaboration with the MET and IRDNC. 'The game guards and I developed our area maps ourselves, using a GPS (Global Positioning System) to mark our own points of reference. We do a number of fixed route patrols and random patrols each month, and fill in forms in relation to our maps. Once a month I collate this data and put it into our computerised database. At present we still use the computer at IRDNC's base camp, but eventually we will have our own in the office.

'The new system will show us our wildlife movements and trends over time, so it's a management tool. The way the system has been set up makes feedback to the conservancy easy. I can print out maps and charts for committee meetings and our annual general meeting.'

Vitalus has shown an aptitude for computer work, and was called on to help set up the same system in conservancies further north.

For Vitalus, whose confidence took a knock when he lost his eye and left school prematurely, the training component of his job has been especially challenging – and fulfilling. He particularly enjoys his annual interaction with 20 or so first-year nature conservation students from the Polytech of Namibia, who spend five days at IRDNC's base camp doing an introductory course in community-based natural resource management.

As one watches Vitalus address the students, fluently answer their questions and then lead a field trip, it is hard to recall the awkward, abrupt young man who until quite recently refused to be seen without sunglasses.

One subject that makes him reticent is Torra's black rhino population. 'Don't write about rhino numbers – this is sensitive, confidential data. But you can mention that we know each of our rhinos individually; we monitor them intensively, and we always know where they are.'

Vitalus and the game guards have proved this on more than one occasion. Some years ago they spotted an ailing rhino, reported it to MET, and monitored it until its death of natural causes; in two other cases they found a rhino carcass within hours after death. Working with MET and NGO staff they were able to rule out foul play.

Monitoring rhino and elephant requires getting close enough to the animal to see distinguishing features such as horn or tusk shapes, ear marks, and so on. This is a skill that Vitalus did not have as a farmer. 'I had to learn how to approach dangerous animals safely, and how to guide visitors up close. It was a responsibility I wasn't keen to take on at first, but people like Colin Nott,

former co-ordinator of IRDNC in Kunene, pushed me. Now I'm very grateful. I have learnt so much in the past few years – my life has opened up.'

He sees the conservancy as a vehicle for development and wealth in his community. It is already a source of self-esteem for many, he says: 'People, including me, are proud of the fact we can make our own decisions about our wildlife. For example, we can shoot a springbok or two from our quota for our annual general meeting; we were able to contribute five springbok to the Namibian independence celebrations at Khorixas and Bergsig this year.'

Something else he is proud of is the fact that Torra's wildlife is calm and unskittish. 'The other night a rhino walked right up to our goats' water trough at the farmhouse. Ostrich and springbok live peacefully with our stock. All our visitors notice this and remark on it.'

In the past 18 months Vitalus and his team have followed up five cases of illegal hunting. Three of the five cases involved outsiders, and in four of those convictions were obtained. The fifth case is still due for trial. He feels strongly that now that

local people have a legal mechanism to obtain rights over huntable game, there is no excuse for poaching.

'I know I speak for the majority in my community. Now that the game belongs to us, we should all benefit together in a planned and sustainable way. It's not fair that one family has to slaughter their own goat for meat while their neighbour is getting free meat from the veld.'

One of few children still at home, and the only one at home with a job, he is the breadwinner on the farm, responsible for his ageing parents – not that he sees much of his family, as he frequently gets home after dark. 'This is probably why he is still a bachelor,' quips one of his colleagues.

Later, after Vitalus has headed off in a cloud of dust in the conservancy's 4x4 in response to a radio message from a game guard, I review my notes from the interview and see that he used the phrase 'my life opened up' three times, in different contexts. I look out over the harsh, rocky plain, filled with the red rocks after which Torra is named, and reflect that life is indeed what you make of it.

Like all of us, Kwazerendu has more than one face. Today she is a dignified matriarch, sitting straight-backed on a goatskin on the ground in the early morning sun outside her hut at *Okozombo* (Place of the Ostrich), about 25 kilometres upriver of Purros. With her are her daughter-in-law, two grand-daughters, and her great-granddaughters – four generations together around a small, smouldering fire.

Typically, the clothing spans three worlds. The youngest girl wears a faded blue and white, store-bought dress; her older cousin, Naminyandi, is regal in her traditional Herero women's headdress and matching grey and purple 'big dress'. Naminyandi's baby sleeps on her back in a leather and metal bead *ondikua* (baby carrier).

Kwazerendu's daughter-in-law is half-dressed, in the manner of a woman at home in the early morning. She wears a sleeveless cotton bodice and long, gathered underdress or petticoat. Later she will pull a big dress over her patched undergarments, adding another 10 metres of cloth to the seven or eight metres she already wears. As usual, Kwazerendu is attired in her wide leather-and-metal bead belt, short calfskin and black *erapi* (cloth) skirts, with her upper body bare except for the large white shell on her chest. On her head is her leather *erembe*.

The old woman's head is bent over the palm frond basket she is weaving. She works with agile fingers while the younger women talk.

If I had not known her for 15 years, it would be easy to believe this is who she is: a quiet, whipcord-thin old woman, content to sit in the sun, making a basket and listening to the chatter of the younger people.

In fact, Kwazerendu is a much respected trance healer; people travel from far and wide to seek out her skills. When she is at work, she leads group trances and acts as the chief exorcist of unwelcome spirits. The contrast between the serene figure at the fire and the frenetic, body-contorting energy she manifests at the climax of a trance is all the more amazing when one considers she must be in her mid- or late 70s.

Kwazerendu does not know exactly how old she is. She was born in north-west Namibia

within 100 kilometres of where she now lives, since the death of her husband, with her son Tjirewe. We estimate her approximate age – around 75 – by working forward from her age-set, *Otjovahona* – meaning 'wealthy people' – up until the latest age-sets.

I ask her what the land means to her; in reply, she points to the dried palm fronds she is transforming into a basket, and then to the green Hoarusib River bed a few hundred metres below us. 'I live from these palms,' she says. Kwazerendu sells up to four baskets a month to passing tourists, earning more than N$250. She uses this income to buy blankets, material, metal beads, domestic utensils and food.

Like most people of Purros, where a community-based conservation project has been in place for more than a decade, she clearly understands the link between tourism and wildlife. She is a member of the Purros Conservancy, and believes 'the work of the conservancy is to protect wildlife and develop

people'. It is a good idea of the government, she observes, to 'give our wildlife back to us'.

Kwazerendu grew up in Kaokoland, as Kunene was formerly known, when wildlife was plentiful and Himba herders judged the health of the land – its capacity to support their cattle – by the condition and number of wild animals thriving in the area. After the worst drought in living memory in the late 1970s and the massive poaching of wildlife up until the mid-1980s, only remnant populations remained. For more than a decade there were no elephants at Purros. The amount of elephant dung encountered as one walks to Purros spring today belies that this hiatus ever existed.

A community game guard network, followed by a tourism levy paid to the resident community as caretakers of the wildlife by two of the many tour operators using Purros, helped to change the situation, and wildlife is returning, especially to Purros with its several linear oases in the Hoarusib River bed.

Kwazerendu's son Tjirewe, who works as a game guard for Purros Conservancy, tells us there are 23 elephants at Purros at present, including a very big bull who is usually found in the bed of the Hoanib River, about 70 kilometres south of Purros's Hoarusib River. His mother says she is too old and her eyesight too poor to see much of anything these days, even elephant, but she enjoys the excitement of the children when elephants or giraffe pass in the river bed below the homestead. 'The children climb up the hill behind us, and shout to their parents what they can see.'

At her age, Kwazerendu does not want much, just that the wildlife and the people continue to live well together, and that the tourists who buy her baskets keep coming. She is also keen that the conservancy committee gets on with their plan to build a traditional Himba village for tourists at *Okongombesemba*, near Purros. This will facilitate the sale of baskets, she believes, as a craft market will be linked to the project.

Her granddaughter, Naminyandi, hopes the conservancy will generate more jobs, thus keeping the young men – including the father of her child – in the area. 'The money the conservancy earns will also be able to help the members if we are hungry or sick.' She is referring to discussions about a drought relief fund. The women agree that the Purros office, due to be built soon and equipped with an HF radio, will greatly assist residents by, for example, enabling them to contact the clinic at Sesfontein or the hospital at Opuwo to organise transport in case of serious illness. Purros is only 100 kilometres by road from Sesfontein, but without a vehicle that is a three-day walk.

Our group has now been joined by some of the men, and the talk flows from the equitable benefit distribution plan of the conservancy back to wild animals and then to *ozombepo* – the 'wind' that is responsible for Kwazerendu's skill as a trance healer. The link between the two

topics is the spirit lion that Kwazerendu recently banished from the body of a possessed woman.

Just as the healing wind entered Kwazerendu's body from that of her late mother, she expects one of her three children to inherit it when she dies. Interestingly, this time she believes it will go to a man, her only son Tjirewe and not to one of her two daughters. My half-joking question – could this be because he is a game guard and knows the ways of wild animals, including presumably spirit lions? – provokes much laughter.

Tjirewe, a man of few words except when the honey beer is plentiful, surprises us all with an insight: conservancies are about wildlife, tourism, jobs and money, but they are also about people's culture. His mother and an older man agree, and he is encouraged to continue. 'Our culture is almost the beginning of this place – where our conservancy was founded. If you take away our culture we will have no history, no past.'

In our group is the conservancy treasurer and field officer, Hiskia Maverara, a young Herero man who went to school and who, unlike the older people, can read and write. What does he think about this talk of culture? He does not disagree with his elders, but his views take him on his own route. He indicates the spectacular river valley in which we sit: 'The conservancy is no different from our farming, and it has brought us young people back to this land. I went away to school and came back knowing little of this area. As a worker for the conservancy, I have had to go out with the older men and learn the land and the wildlife. The wildlife will bring us income but only if we protect it and understand tourism … it comes back to the land.'

Bent over her basket, old Kwazerendu smiles, perhaps because she is warmed by the young man's words. Or perhaps her mind is elsewhere, exploring another landscape, where the spirits of the old people, of long-dead wide-horned cattle and of the great vanished herds of zebra, gemsbok, springbok and elephant still roam.

EHRENS KARUTJAIVA, VICE-CHAIRMAN OF THE PURROS
CONSERVANCY COMMITTEE, HERERO SUB-ELDER,
FARMER

Ehrens's stock camp, to which he and his family moved a few weeks ago, is built on a stony hill above the Hoarusib River, about 20 kilometres upriver of Purros. It comprises four small shelters built of mopane sticks and blue plastic sheeting, and a stick and stone enclosure for kid goats. One wall of the main hut has been plastered with cattle dung, to protect the occupants against the prevailing wind. The view is magnificent, with the pale, bare slopes falling away to the lush, verdant river bed, snaking its way through the desert valley. Opposite, above the Hoarusib's northern banks, rise russet and purple mountains. But the scenery is not the reason why people live high up on the slopes; they perch their homes here to avoid the elephants.

Explains Ehrens: 'The elephants are down there in the river bed where there is water and food. There's no reason for them to come up here, so my people sleep safely. You just have to be very careful not to bump into them by mistake when you're walking in the river to get to the water ...' Ehrens is pragmatic about the dangers of sharing your land with elephants, because he believes the elephants are one of the main drawcards for tourists to the area.

'Our wildlife is our future,' he declares. 'There's nothing else out here that could bring development to a place like Purros.' He is probably right: Purros, about 55 kilometres inland from the Skeleton Coast, is marginal for stock farming except after the occasional good rains once or twice in a decade, and from an environmental point of view should not be permanently settled at all. What enables people to live here, as long as stock is kept mobile, are the permanent springs in the Hoarusib River. This is also what attracts the elephants and other wildlife in the area.

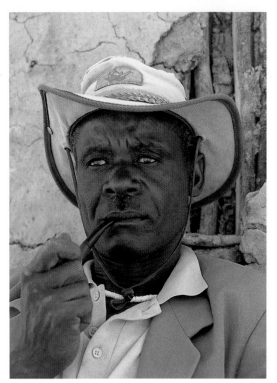

Ehrens formed part of the drive to form a conservancy from the outset. He and his team have just completed all the legal requirements, and their application has been submitted to the government in late October. It was a long, hard road, he says. Agreeing on boundaries with neighbouring communities alone took five months of negotiations.

'But we think all the hard work will be worth it,' he adds. 'We have very high hopes for our conservancy.' The most important challenge, he feels, is to create jobs for the youth; 'there is a lot of employment just waiting here once the conservancy gets going.'

Conservancy members are already at work building a traditional Himba village and craft market for tourists. Their plans also include a campsite and luxury lodge, the latter a joint venture.

[In March 2000 Ehrens and his team heard that their application had been successful. Purros was the 10th communal area conservancy registered.]

Ehrens is very conscious of the role of the conservancy to uplift the community as a whole. In the past, tourism laws allowed private individuals to benefit from running businesses on communal land, with the central government receiving concession or Permission to Occupy fees.

Now, while free enterprise is still encouraged, entrepreneurs are required by law to enter into contracts with conservancies. This could entail rent, or some other form of profit-sharing. Obviously, it is in the interests of the conservancy that the business succeeds and makes a profit, so the contract should take both parties' interests into account. As the committee is a democratically elected body, subject to constitutional checks and balances aimed at ensuring transparency, ordinary conservancy members' interests should be collectively upheld.

These issues have been very much on Erhens's mind, as he and the committee have been locked

Like the rest of north-western Namibia, Purros came close to losing its wildlife during the great drought of the late 1970s and the major poaching wave that accompanied it. Local people, as well as former government officials, were involved. By the early 1980s elephants were completely shot out in the Hoarusib, as were the black rhino.

A community-based conservation project involving community-appointed game guards, followed by a pilot project for sharing the benefits of tourism with Purros residents, helped to change this situation. Elephants have returned to Purros after an absence of a decade, and most other species are doing well. Giraffe were reintroduced to the area by the Ministry of Environment and Tourism, and gemsbok, kudu, springbok and ostrich are common once again.

A logical next step for the community of fewer than 100 adults was to take advantage of the innovative legislative changes of 1996 which gave communal area farmers the same rights as freehold farmers to form conservancies, and thus conditional rights over wildlife and tourism.

in acrimonious discussions with a local businessman – a wealthy Herero herder whose family manages a so-called community campsite at Purros. Although the camp was conceived as a joint venture between the businessman and the local community, the former has more or less run it as his own business for some years. Interestingly, the conflict is not directly about money, as the businessman is prepared to pay a percentage of his profits towards 'community development'. The main grievance of the committee is twofold: firstly, that the businessman refuses to recognise that the conservancy committee has any legal standing, even though the conservancy is about to become registered; and secondly, that the businessman only employs members of his own family.

'This is not fair,' says Ehrens; 'tourists stay in the camp because of the wildlife here. Everyone who farms here protects the wild animals, and we all live with the elephants. Benefits such as jobs should be spread wider than just one family.'

Part of the solution, he believes, is for the conservancy to facilitate another campsite and create more jobs; as the existing campsite is often full in the prime tourist season, a second camp is likely to be economically viable.

The traditional village, another campsite and a craft market will create another dozen or so jobs locally, with the possible increase in craft sales providing additional income, particularly for women and the elderly. 'We are a small community – even 12 new jobs will make a big difference,' says Ehrens. 'We need to keep our young people here, not lose them to big towns where there's no work anyway.'

Ehrens, 49, has experienced the frustrations of seeking work, although in his youth, in the late 1960s and early 1970s, finding jobs was a lot easier than today. Nevertheless, he had to move all over Namibia. He first worked as a labourer at Walvis Bay, and then helped ferry water to a desert tourist camp. His third and last job was doing semi-skilled work at the post office at Arandis, then at Okahandja, and finally at Opuwo.

The occupation of Opuwo by the South African armed forces during SWAPO's liberation struggle sent Ehrens home to Otjindakwe, outside

Sesfontein, where he was born. He trekked to Purros with family stock, and has lived in this area ever since.

His patrilineage herds were completely destroyed during the killer drought of the late 1970s, and although he has a large goat herd he is only just starting to build up his cattle. He has two cows. One of the men with us points out both cows are pregnant, so he might as well say he has four animals. But Ehrens, a cautious man, disagrees – you don't count calves till they are born, he says.

Ehrens's community work is time-consuming, with meetings and other commitments often taking him away from his farming. He was chosen as chairman of the first development committee, a post he held until this committee was transformed into the conservancy committee.

The conservancy, with the potential for jobs and development, has enriched Ehrens's sense of place. He gazes over the river valley: 'This river is our life; each tree is valuable. Look at these hills – you know how they are after rain, green and alive. Walk to the top of that mountain and everything you need to live is there – water,

honey, veld food. If you had to sleep up there tonight you would rest well, with a full belly.

'This land is beautiful and very valuable. We must hold it gently in our hands because our future, our children's future, lies here.

'Now I want to show you where we would like to build a joint venture lodge. It's got the best view in the valley, and good water. All we need is an investor.'

It is time to leave – but there is still time for a cup of tea. Ehrens starts a small fire with a piece of elephant dung and a few twigs. As we wait for the kettle to boil, we watch a row of ostriches picking their way with comic elegance among the rocks on the hills opposite; a herd of goats is visible, as are some graceful springbok. Out of sight in the river bed, elephants are feeding peacefully where their forebears fed. There are giraffe spoor at the nearest spring below us. We can hear distant children's voices … a snatch of a song, ending in laughter. An azure sky arcs above us; for a moment the spirit of optimism and hope in this remote desert community is almost tangible.

Hold this land gently, I think with a full heart, for it does indeed hold the future.

'*The sea, the sea teemed with fish... now there is almost nothing. Formerly the people were never hungry, we made ropes out of tree bark and the fishing hooks were micaia thorns. Others made fish traps with tree roots and reeds. You could catch fish in any manner, but now everything has changed, I don't know whether it's the winds or the temperatures which have dropped, the fish don't want to come in anymore.*' ...

Then the chief stopped thoughtfully, but he finally shook his head.

'*You know, fish are like people, they may be born here at Inhaca but they go and work in South Africa.*'

Chief Nyaka, Inhaca Island (Mozambique)

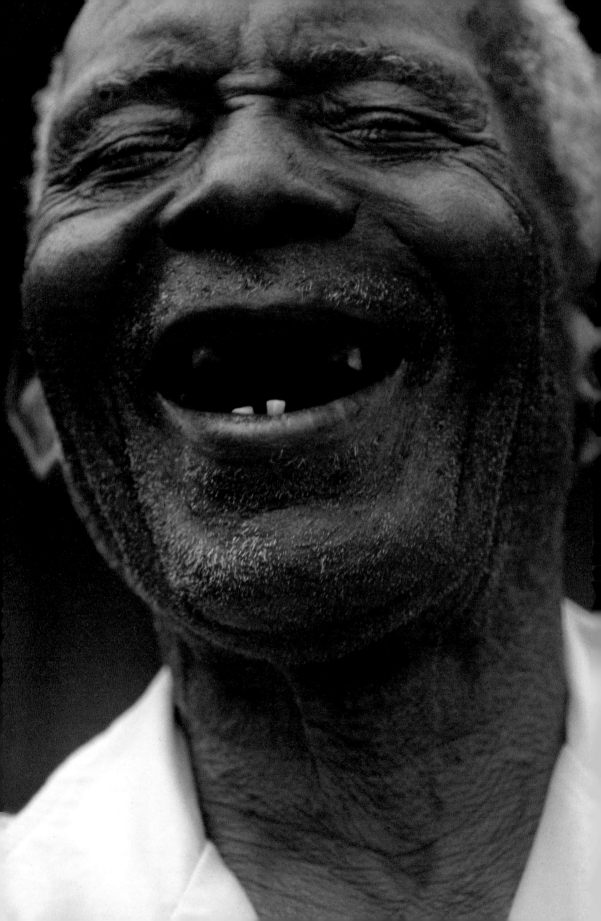

A tale of two islands

Inhaca

By Sérgio Veiga

In view of the great interest in the islands' natural systems, their environmental fragility, their socio-economic reality and in the surrounding sea, it is recommended that their development be based on ecotourism. It will have to be high-quality tourism in order to avoid mass tourism.
Republic of Mozambique, Strategy for the Development of Tourism, 1995-1999.

We have left Maputo, the place that witnessed my birth; with me is the sea, and in front of me the island that witnessed my growth.

It is there where I allow my soul to wander through the horizons of the imagination, where I write my poems and create my paintings. The warm shades and emerald greens of the sea infuse my life with colour.

This is where we are heading. I'm taking a friend with me, so that he may get to know the people who have adopted me. We travel in my motorboat against the waves, against the wind, against time itself. We encounter numerous sailing boats, coming from all directions but all seeming to sail with the waves, as if each owns its own wind.

These dhows are already a living expression of the native people, and our presence here seems out of tune. But we want to hear their folk-tales, and explore their intimate relationship with their habitat.

After 45 minutes the island becomes a reality before our eyes. Mild swells from the channel touch the white sands. Coconut trees are towering above the varied shades of green, and their tops are stirring in the wind.

A little later, we allow the island's enchantment to take hold of us and teach us to give time to time. Sitting on a tree trunk thrown on to the shore, we look back on our course, now gilded by the sun, hiding behind the faded outline of Maputo.

A sailing boat advances towards us, running before the wind. Its sails are patched, like translucent mosaics backlit on a warm afternoon. It cleaves the waves so lightly that it seems as if it wants to avoid waking Inhaca up from its spell, from its myths, from its stories – stories which the wind seems to blow into each remnant of canvas used in the daily bustle of the fisherfolk.

Before the artist's or the poet's eyes, nothing vanishes here; everything is transformed. When the fireball falls asleep and the purple sky is overtaken by the black blue, the nebulae give us a sensation of infinity. The city's lights, and those of the boats moored in the bay, glisten on the water as if they wish to imitate the stars. Denying our desire to see more, we take shelter in my cottage on the beach, hidden among the trees.

We wake up with the dawn, like new men. We lose sight of the dhows in a world of subdued blues, with the horizon dimmed in the haze. Everything seems still. A boat divested of its sails and waiting for its fisherman is reflected in the pool of water that has served as its bed.

Behind the cottage, the dune sand tries to erase the contours of our feet as we walk inland.

Children with books in their hands pass us by, some walking fast, others jogging slowly. Women with baskets are walking in the opposite direction to gather cockles, oysters and other shellfish in the low tide.

The sun rises slowly, getting angry with the indigenous tree which is blocking its rays. In its shadow is a middle-aged man, his muscled body bearing witness to the strenuous work of the sea. I know him well – a vigorous man who lives intensely in the present, puts tomorrow lucidly in perspective, and equally remembers his past. His dark skin contrasts with his name: Albino.

I introduce my friend. Surrounded by fishing lines, sinkers and hooks which he is fixing and unravelling, Albino pretends to get up while greeting us in return. Around his neck is a piece of fishing line, strung with beads seemingly made from fish vertebrae. I turn my curiosity into a question, and let my friend Albino enter the world of his tradition: 'They are boa constrictor's bones, to lessen rheumatism pains.'

I ask him to talk to me about the island's history. He asks in turn: 'Which one of the islands: Nhaca or Inhaca?'

I ask my friend to speak of everything his heart whispers to him in his dreams. He looks at me thoughtfully, and begins:

'Once I exchanged a piece of land for a boat's engine from a Boer. From that day onwards I began to travel far out to fish … I would reach the place where the hotel's recreational fishing boats were. My boat was fragile, but we trusted each other. It knew that not only I was at the helm, but also a whole generation of seafarers who had passed their secrets on to me in the course of time.

'I crossed so many waves, and so many winds carried me, that sometimes I lost the courage to go on. It seemed that I was sailing against the currents of the world itself. I felt I could never reach anywhere, neither I nor my people. But, no matter how tired my soul was, my steady hand continued to hold the helm. It must have been my ancestors protecting me and giving me courage to hold on to life.

'I consulted them on one of those days when only my body was steering my boat; when my spirit wandered along unknown horizons. Perhaps they could explain the reason for my anguish.

'My boat's bow rose and fell in the blue sea. Some time later, as the wind and waves grew stronger, I found a creature flapping on the deck; I couldn't make out whether it was a fish with wings or a bird with scales. As I thought it had come with the waves, and it seemed to be injured, I gave it back to the sea so that the fish could attend to it. But to my amazement the sea returned it to the deck. I thought, perhaps it had been rejected in the fish hospital because of its wings. Afterwards a seagull took it and returned it to me once again. I thought, poor thing, it was also not accepted among the birds; this time its scales had betrayed it. Then I stuck it on a fish

hook to see whether I could catch a shark, as it seemed to me that it was already ill-fated.'

Then Albino lowers his eyes and says sadly:

'On ill fortune run those people who sail in a mulatto boat, between two cultures, where either the wind carries it or the engine thwarts the currents. They are like that flying fish which, no matter how much it flies, will never be like the seagulls. They are like that fish which, when it is hurt, will be thrown into the sea and its fate determined by sharks.

'This is Inhaca, one island within another one, where one culture is encircled by another.'

Albino's words connect us with the mysticism which always seems to hover in the air. Aboard this phantasmic boat, its sails shredded by fables and myths, we allow the wind to take us to the island's roots, travelling through the dreams of men and the straits between the two cultures that separated them. We want to find out whether there were any ways in which those straits were being bridged.

We sail among *mafurreiras* (cashew trees), hemp trees, and many other indigenous trees. In the clearings, mainly in the lower-lying areas, women till the fields where cassava, sweet potatoes and sesame seeds are grown.

We go to see Chief Nhaca. He lives near the heart of the island, at the foot of the highest dune. He lives in a thatched hut, surrounded by others housing the many leaves of the Nhaca family tree. Despite his status he seems to live in dire poverty. Some fruit trees surround the huts. Hanging on a tree are a few oars and a fishing net; a few drums lean against a palisade, and three or four chickens nibble on the ground. His whole life seems to be there, written in these objects.

But there is no one there. After reading the tracks disappearing into the bush, a 12-year-old points seawards and says shyly that Chief Nhaca has gone fishing. The old chief has kept wealth in his soul, as well as the legs of the Nhacas who have walked these dunes for centuries.

We return the next day shortly after dawn, and the old man comes out to meet us. He is about 60 years old, spare of frame but with an imposing air; he seems ready to submit reality to his will for many more years.

As always, the chief greets me as if I am some-one special. No matter how much I am one among others here, fate seems to have blessed my name.

About 30 years ago, a boat sank during a storm off Portuguese Island, claiming the lives of an elderly Nhaca, the spiritual guide of the island, and four youths. A diver also called Sérgio joined the rescue search, but found the youths and old Nhaca already lifeless.

That Sérgio is an old friend, and from him I came to know the details, which he remembered as if time had not gone by.

'It wasn't the first time that I had found men who had lost their lives in the sea,' he said, 'but old Nhaca was different. Whenever I remember it, I feel the shiver I felt that day. He was the last one to be picked up, floating in a vertical position with open arms; he seemed to have died talking to God.'

Sérgio also told me that, after the burials, a prayer was said entreating the ancestors to send rain, so that their blessing might fall on the land and water the *machambas* (cultivated plots). A little later a violent thunderstorm broke out, and it rained the whole night. At dawn everything was peaceful, as if to conceal the response to the prayers.

Those deaths are still commemorated every year at two different sites on the island: one the Nhaca's grave, and the other the first dwelling of the Nhacas at Inguane, now called Santa Maria.

All my attempts to tell people that I was not the same Sérgio have been in vain; the island's older men prefer to believe that I am the same Sérgio in a different guise. At any rate, I share the same love for the island's people and the sea as the other Sérgio and old Nhaca.

Now we are sitting on long benches outside the chief's hut which seem to have stood up to several generations. We understand one another, because we speak the language of the trees and the fish. Speaking in Ronga, the local Shangaan dialect, the old man begins to remember the past:

'In the old days this land was a peninsula connected to Machungulo. There was only a swampy shoal with reeds, and it was there that my great-grandfather crossed. My grandfather was born with the island, and wanted to keep it in the secret of the gods. He kept my ancestors' Nhaca surname and built our house here at the centre of the island, underneath the highest mountain.

'During that time my grandfather sent a message asking chief Maputso to recognise him. In reply, the latter sent his elders to visit the island. Whenever they appeared, Nchaca killed goats, half of which were eaten and the rest of which were taken to the chief. After some time, the elders, observing the prosperity of the Nhacas, became envious and launched successive attacks.

'After my father came Inguane, Nkalane, Hobjane Xiba Homo and other daughters, who were not counted at that time. My grandfather converted those names into surnames and put them in strategic places, and they came to marry among themselves. And in this way he managed to stand up to the enemy.

'At that time a chief was respected, but that is not true today. The state pays me little or no attention. I am even thinking of resigning from the position of chief, because they only come to me when there are problems – otherwise they make and unmake things without consulting me.'

When my limited grasp of Ronga fails me, the chief breaks into Portuguese, and the conversation flows on.

'At that time there was no hunger; everything we planted – maize, mapira, and cashew trees – grew and bore fruit. Now, besides the fact that the land is already tired, wild boars eat the little that manages to grow.'

The old man's eyes grow moist: 'And the sea… the sea teemed with fish… now there is almost nothing. Formerly the people were never hungry; we made ropes out of tree bark, and fish hooks out of *micaia* thorns. Others made fish traps with tree roots and reeds. You could catch fish in any manner, but now everything has changed. I don't know whether it's the winds or the temperatures, but the fish don't want to come in any more.'

I speak to him about the increase in the island's population, mainly due to wartime refugees; of the tired lands; and of all those people having to live off the natural resources and fundamentally off the sea. I also ask him about the commercialisation of fishing, and whether tourism and recreational fishing would have any negative effects.

But in the old seafarer's soul there is no place for selfishness, envy or mistrust; Nhaca believes the sea is an inexhaustible source. He finally shakes his head: 'You know, fish are like people; they may be born here at Inhaca but they go and work in South Africa.'

The following day we sail up to the northern tip of Inhaca, where a lighthouse stands on top of

a dune. We climb winding stairs within the cement cylinder up to a door which opens on to a circular verandah. From there one can see the whole island.

From the lighthouse down to the south stretches a chain of dunes which, protected by dense indigenous vegetation, stands up to the eastern and southern winds. At its edges, where it is exposed to the turbulent sea, the island has had to protect itself against damage by generating rocky surfaces.

Inland, the dunes soften into a flatter surface which fades into the Inhaca Bag, a long underwater valley which ends in the narrow strait separating the island from the mainland and extends into sandbanks and mango groves towards the island's interior.

The dune that supports the lighthouse falls away into a plain where coconut trees shelter a fishing village, and spread out until they touch the sea. A calm bay separates Inhaca from Portuegese Island. In the shallows, mango groves serve as a shelter for fishing vessels; where they widen, sinuous inlets penetrate leafy recesses. These harbour a diverse number of birds, and also serve as fish breeding zones.

Another Nhaca, David Xaicomo, lives in a house in that village, which looks out at the sunsets behind Portuguese Island. He is the same age as the coconut trees that overshadow him. His brush has only been guided by his soul; a naïve artist, he has painted a wide variety of subjects from the queen of England and Marshall Carmona to the luxurious yachts of Miami, which bring him back to the dhows of his own culture.

We feel only his body is with us, because when the sun slumbers he keeps up with it in sleep and his soul flies beyond normal borders.

He is a traveller, because this is what his ancestors have dictated. His father was an Nhaca called Xaia Homo, which means 'strike the bull' in Shangaan. When he left for South Africa his

name was changed to the Zulu Xaia N'komo, which eventually turned into Xaicomo. When he returned, having broadened his cultural horizons, he fell into the good graces of the colonial government, which granted him the status of chief of Portuguese Island.

Like someone who challenges fate, he baptised his eldest daughter as Luck; she married a male nurse who worked at the island's medical post and who, years later, became the first president of Mozambique.

Later still, in the newly independent Mozambique, the status of chief was taken away from him and returned to the original Nhaca lineage. But the island of the Portuguese ended up by freeing his soul, because it was there during a storm, in a meeting of tides, that a boat Xaicomo was in sank… and this was the body my friend Sérgio recovered.

At dawn the following morning, with the wind hardly stirring, we wake up with singing coming from the sea. A hazy layer covers the sun, creating a silver filtered light.

Waist-deep in water, a priest in white garments and with a cross embroidered on his chest opens his arms and his soul to the sea. He is surrounded by a dozen believers; with wailing voices, from the depths of their souls, they re-enact a religious ceremony in which a woman was cruelly immersed in the salt waters to be released from evil spirits. They are Maziones, a religious group who believes that God's blessing comes from the sea, because they say that Christ, by having been baptised in water, left his blessing there.

Many other religions exist on the island, but like the trees planted in the sandy dunes none has yet managed to prosper. Despite the proximity of the country's capital, not even in colonial times did the Catholic Church, so strongly supported by the government, manage to establish itself there. There is no memory of any chapel being built. It is as if the imported culture in the city submerged its arms in water and allowed the indigenous people's hands to emerge from the other side of the bay – hands which still cast lots with bones and shells, to be wisely read by witchdoctors.

In the Bag, among tall shrubs and a maze of intersecting paths, we arrive at the hut where Muamikava lives. I take off my shoes and sit down in front of her, in the place reserved for me. A west-facing window lets in the light of the setting sun, and lights the stones where the ancestors' knowledge is written. The woman of the spirits whirls the shells, and slowly answers the silent questions I hold in my mind. There are gaps in the spaces where she tries to decipher the past and discern the future. But I only remember the moments that coincide with the truth.

One day, a long time ago, an Nhaca and an Nhamussoro climbed the island's highest dune, looked over the sea and blessed it, imparting different features to various parts of the island and its coastline.

This is because the sea is an enchanted mirror, which reflects the face of whoever wants to disturb its intimacy. In the daytime it is heavenly, because it reflects the sky; at nighttime it dresses in silver, and serves as mirror to the moon. It only shows what it is hiding under the mirrored mantle when it allows itself to be loved. Then it undresses in the fading blues of the bottom of the sea, where coral and seaweed gardens provide a stage for the gods in a contest of the most diversified life forms and colours. As if miraculously, each habitat transforms itself when faced with changes in temperatures, depths and ocean.

In the Indian Ocean surrounding Inhaca – more accurately in Inguane, the strait that turns it into an island – the sea floor's characteristics are gradually transformed as it expands towards the Bag. The choppy waters become crystal clear at high tide, and sharks, giant *xaréus* and other big fish look for food in the inner bay.

Closer in, a reef that falls vertically down to a depth of 10 metres protects the island against strong currents. It is like an inner frontier, where sharks are forbidden entry and only giant xareus and barracudas dare invade. Lastly, through a shallow strait fading into the Bag, a coral reef

protects small tropical fish. Where the floor finally opens up into the Bag, mango groves spring up, providing a breeding ground for various marine species and nourishment for dugongs. Near the shore, which slopes down in a red cliff, is another coral barrier. These coral reefs are considered to be among the southernmost in the hemisphere.

The island has different fauna and flora, on land and in the sea, because it is a conflict zone between tropical warm currents and colder waters.

At depths of between 10 and 30 metres giant groupers and other sedentary fish welcome the travelling shoals looking for a place to stay overnight. In the open sea, on the rocky floors, a few corals grow spontaneously, and the seaweeds hide the memories of ships sunk during World War 2 and of others wrecked on the shallow reefs. The marlins, *veleiros* and other pelagic fish are the main settlers of those crystal waters.

But in all those places, when night falls, everything changes. The sedentary fish take shelter and sleep, and are replaced by other fish which remained underneath the rocks during the day. Some corals bloom, and in the high seas sharks slice through the dark blue looking for food.

No matter how well I know the sea, it seems it wants to tell me more. Perhaps, in its mystical simplicity, it wants to show me how much evil my brothers have done to it.

If this is my sea, and if these are the people of the island who have adopted me, then Vasco is my brother. Born on the island, he did not sail in a boat with shredded sails, because he wasn't a sailor, but he certainly hovered for a long time, with patched pants, over the stormy waves of the sea of cultures separating the two islands.

At age 12 he stopped climbing coconut trees, because he believed he could climb the highest tree of the other, fictitious, island. He looked at the top and grabbed the lowest branch ... he started working at the hotel as a messenger boy. He studied, earned the trust of his superiors, and at 35 became hotel director. His mission is to ensure the success of Pestana Hotels and Resorts and,

more important, to build the bridge that will link one island with the other.

The group supports local communities in every way it can, from paying a monetary amount to the administration to providing free electricity to the hospital. The production of crafts for sale to tourists has been encouraged, and a local dance school is being formed to perform on festive days. The hotel employs about 80 people born on the island, and buys not only local fish but also everything the small farmers can supply.

But this is a drop in the ocean. Given the rate of population growth, any revenue arising from tourist activity will be increasingly insufficient. Development plans centred on tourism can only work if population growth rates are lowered.

How can a hotel, how can anyone help an island's population of more than 6 000? All the support that can be given – and employment is the most significant – will increasingly be merely symbolic. The bridge built between the two cultures will result in greater benefits for the company, whose main objective is to make a profit.

But for director Vasco Manhiça, like the sailor who, fastened to the boat's helm, fights against winds and tides, hope dies last. These tourist institutions, he says, should take extreme care to minimise their impact on the environment, especially in such sensitive places as Inhaca.

I have been bonded to the sea for 25 years. As short a period as that may be in a world that has survived so many millennia, I have observed a significant degradation in that period of time. What will it be like in another 25 years' time?

While researching this article, I interviewed islanders of all ages. Everybody agrees that there are fewer marine resources. *Oluturias* are almost extinct, and I haven't seen any dugongs for more than five years. As for the fish themselves, if there are still giant groupers in the deep gorges close to the island it's because my speargun is tired and I have taught it to kill like the islanders' *gamboas* (fish traps): only to feed me.

But nobody believes the decrease in marine species is connected to human activity. Are people indeed deluded by sporadic catches which make them believe that, one day, everything will be back to normal? A surprising case occurred in mid-June, when I was on the island writing this article. A shoal of tuna was caught between two sand-banks at low tide, allowing a fisherman to catch 47 tuna weighing on average 20 kilograms each. This was most unusual, firstly because tuna fish is a summer fish and also because their average weight in Inhaca waters is 10 kilograms.

Will Inhaca's marine resources disappear? Or will people be afraid to face reality, fearing to be the victims of restrictions in the short term?

If there had been no Western interference, and if the people of Africa had continued to capture species with their own means and for their own subsistence, would its fauna and flora still have been endangered?

With the southern wind blowing strongly, I fall exhausted into bed, and my subconscious takes over. I dream that the island's old men drag their tired feet and climb up the highest dune so that they can consult their ancestors together. Afterwards, with stiff hands, each one picks up a spade, tears down the cement walls built on the island, and throws the blocks into the sea. On the second day, they plough the land and planted trees. On the third day, they have in their hands all the fishing gear that has come from the other side of the sea, and set them on fire. When the southern wind passes, the fourth day dawns peacefully, the sun shines warmly, and God had offered as a gift to the island a sea teeming with fish.

The sun rises, and the light breaks through the window of my cottage. I wake up distressed, because despite being the child of someone who was born here I feel like an adopted son of Africa. But everything is the same: the waves fall in a calm seesaw on the beach, and the crabs follow their movement, running backwards to avoid being caught by the waves.

Behind the crabs a youth passes with his books in his hand, heading for school. He wants to arrive before the bell rings.

I have to believe in the human being, and in the proverb which says that the crab walks backwards. I believe in that child who, with his books under his arm, is preparing to add the knowledge inherited from his parents and grandparents to the learning provided by the school.

After everything I have seen and heard, I meditate on what that child might think when he makes his own contribution to mankind, and I dare to predict his thoughts.

' ... My grandfather taught me to believe in our ancestors, in witchcraft, in the direction given by our spiritual guides. From afar came other cultures and other religions which led me to believe that those forces are only one and is called God. Who is going to guide the future of my island? My ancestors' spirits? That God? Him and men? Or just men?

'Will we be part of nature just like any other animal, and will there be a spiritual omnipotence that will always balance nature? Or will we be part of that force? In this case, just like the seafarers, we will have to learn how to read the waves and the winds so that we can coexist together.

'Are wars, natural catastrophes or even epidemics telling us something? The Black Plague killed half the world's population in the Middle Ages; now AIDS may do the same in this corner of Africa. It's difficult to imagine Inhaca, Europe, or even the world with three or four times its population. Isn't birth control the solution to the world's huge problem? Will it not be better not to allow birth rather than to see death?

'But if nothing happens by chance, and if the helm of this ship in such stormy seas is in our hands, perhaps one day we will understand the evil caused to nature by technology. But it will also be that same technology that will rebuild it, replant it and resettle it. And if the African continent is the least affected now, it may also be the last one to be rebuilt ...'

The sun is still weak; it has just risen. The calm seesaw of the rising tide wipes out the tracks left by the youth on his way to school. I allow my eyes to wander over the sea. Shoals of mullets are leaping about in fans, avoiding the pursuit of larger fish. On the horizon, in contrast with the city's dim outline, the islanders' sailing boats are slowly fleeing into the wind.

The island of Inhaca is still like this...

About the contributors

Photo: Tony Weaver

Paul Weinberg is a South African-based freelance photographer with a special interest in indigenous people and their environment. His photographs have appeared in magazines in South Africa, the United States and Europe, in local and international exhibitions, and in photographic books and anthologies. He has written and photographed *In search of the San* (1997, The Porcupine Press*)*, a portrayal of surviving San communities throughout southern Africa, and has photographed *Shaken roots* (1990, EDA Publications), a book on the Bushmen of Namibia, and *Back to the land* (1996, The Porcupine Press), documenting the return of rural communities in South Africa to land they had lost under apartheid. In 1993 he won the Mother Jones International Documentary Award for his portrayal of the fisherfolk of Kosi Bay on South Africa's northern Natal coast.

Dr Dhyani Berger is a community conservation facilitator and trainer who has spent most of her life living and working in East Africa. She is particularly well known for her pioneering work among the Maasai, aimed at securing the return of wildlife use rights to indigenous communities. Ultimately, her activities helped to trigger major changes in government policy, leading to the establishment of a community wildlife service in Kenya. Her book *Wildlife extension – participatory conservation by the Maasai of Kenya* (1993, ACTS) documents her early work with the Maasai, aimed at helping them to manage their environment and benefit from wildlife and tourism via partnerships with the government and the private sector.

She is presently working on a WWF project aimed at strengthening Namibia's community-based natural resource management programme.

Besides her work in Africa, she has consulted to various rural development initiatives in Asia and the United States.

Chenjerai Hove is a Zimbabwean born novelist, poet and human rights campaigner. He is a teacher by profession. Hove is the author of several poetry collections and has written three novels, including *Bones and Shadows*. He is also the author of a body of work called *Guardians of our Soil* which celebrates the voice of people living on the land in Zimbabwe. Much of his work is based and rooted in the social fabric of his country. He has lectured widely and internationally about his own work and African literature and poetry as well. He is the recipient of the Noma Awards for literature.

Dr Margaret Jacobsohn is a Namibian writer and social scientist. For the past 15 years she has lived and worked in remote areas in rural Namibia, seeking ways of linking rural development to conservation. She is co-director of the Namibian non-government organisation Integrated Rural Development and Nature Conservation (IRDNC), which works closely with the WWF, as well as of the WorldWide Fund for Nature/DFID Kunene Community-Based Natural Resource Management Project. She has been widely published, and has won several international awards.

Photo: Lyle Owen Smith

Antjie Krog is a South African journalist, writer and poet. She has published eight volumes of poetry, two volumes of verse for children, a short novel published by Heinemann, and a book, *Country of my skull* (Random House, 1998) dealing with the South African Truth and Reconciliation Commission. Her first play was performed in South Africa this year. She has won numerous literary prizes in South Africa and abroad. She has addressed audiences in Europe and the United States, and has lectured on aspects of the Truth and Reconciliation Commission at various European universities. She frequently appears on radio and television programmes in Europe and the United States and also regularly participates in events for poets in Europe. Her works have been translated into English, Dutch, Italian, French and Spanish.

Gcina Mhlope was born in South Africa and is an award winning actress, writer, poet and storyteller. She has performed and published locally and internationally and holds two honorary doctorates in literature. She won the 'obie' award for best actress in *Born in the RSA*, and Josep Jepherson Award for best actress in *Have You Seen Zandile*. She has won the 'Bookchat Award' and 'Carl Lohan' Award for children stories. In 1999 she was awarded the Arts and Culture Heritage award for her contribution to the genre of story telling.

Victor Munnik is a South African journalist specialising in issues surrounding natural resources and sustainable development. He currently edits the magazine *Land & Rural Digest*, and serves as communications manager at a South African rural development NGO, the EDA Trust. Previously, he was a founder member of the independent Afrikaans weekly *Vrye Weekblad*, and deputy editor of the magazine *New Ground*. He has published a book of short stories, written a TV documentary on the ancient African city of Mapungubwe, and published many articles on rural development, water, conservation and the environment.

Paul Ntiati is a Kenyan conservationist and rural development expert. He currently heads the community conservation programme of the African Conservation Centre (ACC). He has also worked with African Wildlife Foundation (AWF) and the Kenya Wildlife Service (KWS) as a field programme co-ordinator, Campfire Conservation (Kenya) as a project leader, the Maasai Rural Training Centre as an extension manager, and the Kenyan Ministry of Agriculture and Livestock Development as a range officer. He has a wealth of experience in community wildlife conservation initiatives.

Sérgio Veiga is a Mozambican writer and artist. He staged his first exhibition at age 17 in Lourenço Marques, now Maputo. Due to the influence of his father, a professional hunter, his works mainly depicted African wildlife scenes. Wildlife remained the subject of his work, also because he became a professional hunter himself. Besides hunting he has also devoted himself to angling, diving and underwater fishing, and marine subjects regularly feature in his work.
He owns a cottage on Inhaca Island, where each sunset is a source of inspiration to him. Side by side with his hunting and fishing activities he has always continued to paint, giving form to his experiences. His paintings are held in various private collections in Mozambique and abroad.

Tony Weaver is a South African freelance photojournalist. He started in journalism in 1981 as a war and political correspondent for South African newspapers. By the mid-1980s he was covering southern Africa for the BBC's African Service, Irish Radio, Radio New Zealand, and the Canadian Broadcasting Corporation's (CBC) National Television News. In 1992 he and his partner, documentary filmmaker Liz Fish, embarked on a two-year journey through central, east and north east Africa which inspired a large volume of work reflecting the people of Africa and their environment. Tony is a contributing editor to *Out There* magazine and writes a weekly current affairs column for the Cape Town morning newspaper *The Cape Times*. He has won numerous awards.

Guide to places visited

All the following projects (ecotourist destinations) are linked directly to the communities who are part of this book. The communities connected to these projects are beneficiaries of joint ventures between local people and tourist companies. The nature of these projects obviously varies from place to place and country to country. It needs to be pointed out that this is not a comprehensive list of all community tourism in the continent but is an up-to-date inventory of the tourist ventures that will link you to the people and places visited in this book.

Botswana
Ecotourist ventures with the Nharo speaking (San) communities of Botswana

Qae Qare Game Farm
PO BOX 219
Ghnazi
Botswana
Tel / fax 267 596285/596244
Email: berg@info.botswana

Kenya
Ecotourist ventures with the Maasai

Moses Kipelian
PO BOX 527
Narok
Kenya

Richard Bonham Safaris
PO BOX 24133
Nairobi
Kenya
Tel 254 2 882521/884475/883449
Fax 254 2 882728
Email: Bonham.Luke@swiftkenya.com

Kibo Slopes Safaris
PO BOX 58064
Nairobi
Kenya
Tel 254 2 725 435/717 373
Fax 254 2 716028
Email: kibo@nbnet.co.ke

Amboseli Communities Wildlife Conservation
and Tourism Project
and Eselenkei Wildlife Reserve
c/o Porini Eco Tourism Ltd,
Freshfield House,
Forest Row,
Sussex RH 185 ES
England
Tel 44 1342 821 011
Fax 44 1342 822 364
Email: lovatsmith@mistral.co.uk

There are also a number of more informal community based ecotourist projects that can be contacted via Paul Ntiati, email pntiati@acc.or.ke

Mozambique

Eco tourist ventures with the Ronga speaking people of Inhaca Island

Inhaca Lodge
Pestana Carlton Hotel
Rua Da Se 114
Caixa postal 4376
Maputo
Mozambique
Tel 258 1 760 010
Fax 258 1 760 011
Email: pestana_resv_moz@hotmail.com

Sérgio Veiga
Bairro do Triomfo
1 st Avenue 166
Maputo
Mozambique
Tel 258 (1) 450 146
Cell 082 306 728

Namibia

Ecotourist ventures with the Nama/Damara, Himba and Herero communities of the Damara and Kunene regions of Namibia

Damaraland Camp
c/o Wilderness Safaris
Email: wildrsa@iafrica.com

Integrated Rural Development and Nature
Conservation (IRDNC)
PO BOX 9681
Windhoek,
Namibia
Tel 264 61 22 85 30
Fax 264 61 22 85 06/9
Email: irdnc@iafrica.com.na

Eco tourist ventures with the San of Namibia

Tsumkwe Lodge
Tel 264 64 20 3581
Fax 264 67 220060

Nyae Nyae Conservancy
PO BOX 9026
Eros
Windhoek
Namibia
Tel 264 61 236 327
Fax 264 61 225 997
Email: nndfn@iafrica.com.na

Nacobta (Namibia Community based Tourism
Ascociation)
PO BOX 86099
Windhoek
Namibia
Tel 264 (o) 61 250558
Fax 264 (o) 61 222647

South Africa

Eco tourist ventures with the Nama speaking people, and the Leliefontein and Ecksteenfontein communities of Namaqualand

Richtersveld National Park
SA National Parks
PO BOX 787
Pretoria 0001
South Africa
Tel 27 12 343 1991
Fax 27 12 343 0905

Kuboes Community Tourist Camp
PO BOX 55
Kuboes 8292
South Africa
Tel 27 27 83 11185
Fax 27 27 83 11322
Email: kubpof@kingsley.co.za

Floors Strauss
c/o Transform (Cultural and community organisation)
PO BOX 406,
Alexander Bay 8290
South Africa
Tel/fax 27 27 83 11417
Cell 083 457 1976

The Zulu-speaking communities of KwaZulu Natal living around the Greater St Lucia Wetland Park Area

c/o KwaZulu Conservation Services
PO BOX 13069
Cascades 3202
South Africa
Tel 27 33 84 51 000
Email: smathap@kznncs.org.za
Website: www.rhino.org.za

Phinda Game Reserve
PO BOX Private Bag X27
Benmore 2010
South Africa
Tel 27 11 809 4300
Email: reservations@ccafrica.com

Zulu Eco Adventures
27 35 4744919. Cell 082 492 6918
Email: eshowe@zululand.co.za
Website: www.zululand.co.za/eshowe

Zimbabwe
Ecotourist ventures with the Shangaan and Shona-speaking communities of Mahenye and Masoka

Mahenye Safari Lodge
Private Bag 7013
Chiredzi
Tel 263 131 3159

Campfire
c/o The Africa Resources Trust
PO BOX HG 960,
Highlands
Harare
Zimbabwe
Tel 263 4 732625
Fax 263 4 739 163
Email: clippai@aol.com

For more information about these destinations please contact:

Great Escape Travel
PO BOX 51246
Musgrave 4062
Durban, South Africa
Tel 27 31 202 4027
Fax 27 31 201 8152
Email: banuk.get@ghalileosa.co.za

Acknowlegements

This project is in the true sense a collaborative one. It could not have happened without a number of forces coming together. Firstly we wish to thank DANCED of South Africa, for their commitment and support for the primary collection of material. This seed money helped the writers, photographer and researchers on their many journeys into the heart of Africa. EDA and in particular Victor Munnik who played a very constructive role in facilitating the meeting of minds between writers, publishers and role players. Novib for their belief and faith in Africa, its people and some of its creative spirits. Jan Mets and Victor Levie who went beyond the call of duty in making this book possible, earning themselves the accolade of 'Blues Brothers'. Riaan de Villiers for his steady hand in crafting the copy. Sue Armstrong for her enthusiasm and participation in the formation of the project. And David Fig for his in-depth knowledge he was willing to share.

There are many organisations who were generous in their participation in this project. In particular we wish to express our gratitude to the South African National Parks Board, Kuru, Nyae Nyae Farmers Co-op, IRDNC, IUCN Mozambique, Campfire Group Ranch Committee (Kenya) and Kibo Slopes Safari. A number of individuals stand out for walking the extra mile with us. Kenneth Nashuu, Nancy Kireu and Joyce Nasieku who shared many days in providing us with an insight into the Kenyan experience. Vasco Manhiça who facilitated and assisted with extensive trips in Inhaca Island. Arno Oosthuisen of Tsumkwe Lodge who helped us out with mechanical problems when we really needed it deep in the Kalahari. Heleen Verwey needs to be thanked for being wonderfully supportive on a number of tough 4x4 trips into the hinterland.

Finally, without countless local people who opened their hearts and homes to us and who have our sincere thanks, this book could never have happened. Under difficult circumstances and with a great deal of grace Africa's indigenous people endure. It is with great appreciation that we were able to journey into their environments and lives to share some of their experiences.

The Authors

Captions

ISBN 90 5330 301 4

NUGI 470/672/829/922

Editor
Riaan de Villiers

Book design
Victor Levie, Amsterdam (NL)

Print
Waanders, Zwolle (NL)